deep comedy

Trinity,
Tragedy,
& Hope
in Western Literature

Peter J. Leithart

CANON PRESS
Moscow, Idaho

Peter J. Leithart, *Deep Comedy: Trinity, Tragedy, and Hope in Western Literature*
© 2006 by Peter J. Leithart

Published by Canon Press, P.O. Box 8729, Moscow, ID 83843
800-488-2034 / www.canonpress.org
Printed in the United States of America.

Cover design by David Dalbey.

06 07 08 09 10 11   9 8 7 6 5 4 3 2 1

Library of Congress Cataloging-in-Publication Data

Leithart, Peter J.
  Deep comedy : trinity, tragedy, and hope in western literature / Peter J. Leithart.
     p. cm.
  Includes bibliographical references and index.
  ISBN 1-59128-027-3
  1. Religion and literature. 2. Christianity and literature. 3. Tragedy—History and criticism. 4. Christianity—Essence, genius, nature. I. Title.

  PN49.L435 2004*
  809'933823—dc22

                            2004018380

To MargaretAnn

Remember that tempests are kind

Contents

Acknowledgments

At times, glory cuts through the mundane like water in the desert. As a long day fades, a weary farmer brings his combine to the top of a hill and finds himself bathed in the blended light of moonrise and sunset. Tracing a footnote in a dusty library basement, a scholar makes a discovery that fundamentally alters the direction of his research, and perhaps the direction of his field. Trudging through an endless round of diaper-changing, child-watching, dish-washing and clothes-washing and everything-else-washing, a mother stops in wonder as her infant daughter takes her first steps.

Such experiences provide some support for the comic vision of reality that I sketch in this book, and, suitably enough, the book originated out of such an experience. Perhaps there are teachers who go into raptures at the thought of grading a stack of papers, but for myself grading is drudgery. Normally, that is. This book, however, originated during a late evening of grading. Scattered through the stack that night were three papers by three different students—Laura Blakey, Michelle Lano, and Hannah Griffith, each of whom developed very similar insights concerning the relationship between ancient heroism and the jolly heroism of Sir Gawain. As I graded those papers, several years of teaching a Western literature survey clicked into place, and the notion of "deep comedy" took form in my mind. The heavens opened, angels descended singing, and a bright light illuminated the room. I am grateful to those students, and to the many others who have contributed to this book in ways that I can no longer retrace.

Thanks to Randy Wood and Randy Compton of Lee University, Cleveland, Tennessee, who invited me to give the Humanities Lecture in the spring of 2004. I used the occasion to present the essentials of the argument in this book, and I was blessed by the interaction with the "Randys" that followed.

Portions of chapters 1, 2, and 4 have been previously published as "Supplement at the Origin: Trinity, Eschatology and History," *International Journal of Systematic Theology*, vol. 6, no. 4 (2004), and that material is used here with the permission of Blackwell Publishers. Thanks to Douglas Jones for his willingness to publish the book, and to Canon Press assistant editor Jared Miller for diligently pressing me to provide actual page numbers in my footnotes.

This book is dedicated to my third daughter, MargaretAnn, who at five exemplifies as well as anyone I know what it means to live out of and in deep comedy. She is a constant source of amusement, with her bizarre, frequently gruesome stories, her prankishness, her wildly expressive eyes. More importantly and profoundly, she exudes the childlike confidence and careless freedom that comes from knowing all will be well, and all manner of things will be well. And with her on my lap or in my arms, I am reassured that it will.

Introduction:
A Roadmap of the Argument

Portions of this book are dense and will be obscure to some read-ers. In order to guide the reader through these dangerous and dimly lit valleys and caverns, this introduction provides a (sketchy) map of where you are heading. You might find the destination is not worth the risks or labors of the journey, and in that case you may, as Lem-ony Snickett would say, put down this book and find something more pleasant to read.

The thesis of this essay grows out of two observations, both of which, particularly the first, will require detailed defense in the pages that follow. Viewed as a whole, firstly, the Christian account of history is eschatological not only in the sense that it comes to a definitive and everlasting end, but in the sense that the end is a glorified be-ginning, not merely a return to origins. The Christian Bible moves *not* from garden lost to garden restored, but from garden to garden-city. God gives with interest. To say the same in other words, though the Bible gives full recognition to sin and its effects on creation and humanity, the Christian account of history is ultimately comic. The classical world, by contrast, was dominated by a tragic view of his-tory, in which history moved from a glorious beginning toward a tar-nished end, and a tragic understanding of the constituent realities of life (a "tragic metaphysics"), manifested in a predominantly tragic literature. As it penetrated the Greco-Roman world, the Christian gospel challenged this tragic classicism (or classical tragicism) by presenting a fundamentally comic vision of history.

"Tragedy" is used here (at least initially) very loosely, as a story in which the characters begin neutrally or well, but slide inexorably to a bad end; "comedy" is a story in which the characters may face dangers, perhaps dangers of great intensity, but ultimately rise to a happy ending. "Deep comedy" brings two additional nuances: First, in deep comedy the happy ending is uncontaminated by any fear of future tragedy, and, second, in deep comedy the characters do not simply end as well as they began, but progress beyond their beginning. Comedy may move from glory to glory restored, but deep comedy moves from glory to added glory. While the classical world did produce comedy, it did not produce "deep comedy."

What I mean by "tragedy" and "deep comedy" may best be captured by two biblical citations. "The last state is worse than the first"—Jesus' saying can serve as a summary of ancient sensibility about history. "Deep comedy" is best exemplified by the vision of the New Jerusalem in Revelation 21–22, and particularly by Revelation 21:4: "He shall wipe away every tear from their eyes; and there shall no longer be death; there shall no longer be mourning, or crying, or pain; the first things have passed away."

My second observation is more straightforward: The Christian God is a triune God. This stands in contrast to all other forms of monotheism and polytheism, ancient and modern.

This small book is an effort to discern a connection between these two unique or at least highly idiosyncratic features of Christian faith. Is Christianity eschatologically comic *because* it is trinitarian? Is history moving toward a comic climax as a revelation of the nature of the triune God? To ask the question from the other end: Is there an "eschatological moment" in the life of the Trinity? Is the life of the Trinity comic? In this book, I sketch the outlines of an affirmative answer to these questions. If trinitarian theology is an answer to the question, "Given the gospel story, who must God be for this to be possible?" I wish to broaden the question beyond the narrative of Jesus' life, death and resurrection to ask, "Given the biblical vision of history and eschatology, who must God be for this to be possible?" The answer is the same in both cases: the immanent Trinity is manifested in and is the ontological ground and condition for the possibility not only of the death and resurrection of the Son, but of a world-history that moves from Eden to New Jerusalem. Paganism's tragic view of history is allied with a tragic metaphysics and theology, while Christianity has a comic view of history because it has a fundamentally comic theology proper (doctrine of God).

The argument proceeds in several stages. Part I examines a single but popular classical myth of history, Hesiod's myth of the "four (or five) ages," to show that the classical world had a predominantly tragic notion of history. In contrast, the biblical conception of history, particularly as evidenced in the prophetic literature of the Old Testament and the New Testament, is predominantly comic. Scripture teaches that history does not degenerate from life to death but is translated from the reign of death into the reign of life.

In Part II, the argument shifts from an historical / mythological plane to a metaphysical / theological plane. I show that for Greek philosophy tragedy was woven into the fabric of existence, and also that these tragic obsessions are common elements of modern and postmodern thought as well. This discussion will be transposed into a more directly theological key as I examine Jacques Derrida's treatment of the problems of writing and supplementarity, especially as they arise in Plato, to point out similarities between ancient conceptions of history and "Platonic" metaphysics and theology. As Derrida shows, it is axiomatic for Plato that supplementarity is degenerative; that is, anything added to an original, anything flowing from a source, is "worse" than the source itself, precisely because it has moved away from the source. This metaphysical assumption is parallel to mythical views of history for which *temporal* supplementation necessarily means degeneration. For Platonic and Neoplatonic metaphysics, the lower is always lesser; for Hesiod, Ovid, and other myth-historians the later is always lesser. Such a metaphysics cannot support a comic view of history, much less deep comedy.

Postmodern atheist though he was, Derrida opened the way for a trinitarian response to the problem of supplementarity by treating the relationship between speaker and text, and between origin and supplement more generally, as a father-son relation. Derrida's father-son, however, is heretical or even pagan, rewriting Hesiod's myth of patricidal Zeus and Sophocles' story of Oedipus as if it were metaphysically necessary. An orthodox trinitarian theology avoids the problematics of Platonic supplementarity in two ways. First, orthodox trinitarian theology asserts that there is always a "supplement" (Son and Spirit) with the "origin" (Father), and, second, insists that the Son and Spirit, though "supplemental" to the Father, are "equal in power and glory." There is no degeneration or "leakage" of glory or divinity as the Father begets the Son or, together with the Son, spirates the Spirit. trinitarian theology thus provides theological ground for a view of history where the passage of time does not necessarily mean decay, where history can move from death to life rather than the (common-sensical) reverse. Thus, for a trinitarian theology, time and history can be redeemed and brought to comic conclusion. For trinitarian theology, the "Second" is fully equal to and is in fact the glory of the "First," and therefore for the Bible, the golden age is always out before us not behind us. Here, as elsewhere, the dominical axiom about protology and eschatology subverts the common sense of antiquity and modernity: "the last first and the first last" (πρωτοι εσχατοι και εσχατοι πρωτοι, Mt. 19:30).

Part III, finally, sketches the effects that the Christian comic vision of history and the Christian comic confession of the triune God had on the shape and tone of Western literature. I return to the classical world to show that, even in its most comic manifestations (the *Odyssey* and *Aeneid* in particular), classical literature never arrived at "deep comedy." Even comically-shaped classical epics, dramas, and stories of the ancient world are overshadowed by the fear of death (cf. Hebrews 2:14–15). Christendom, imperfectly to be sure, has produced a literature characterized by "deep comedy." With the fall of Rome, tragedy virtually disappeared for the better part of a thousand

years. Meanwhile, heroes of medieval romance refused to wait for
adventure to be thrust upon 'em; they sought it out, gladly and con-
fidently. Contrary to the caricature of dourness and dullness, medieval writers produced a rich literature of parody and travesty. Tragedy
was reintroduced in the late medieval period and especially in the
Renaissance, but by then it had been irrevocably contaminated by
Christian hope. The gulf that divides ancient and Renaissance comedy and tragedy is unfathomable. I end the book by examining two
of Shakespeare's plays: *Twelfth Night* manifests the profundity of
Shakespearean "deep comedy," while *King Lear*, Shakespeare's least
hopeful play, shows how far tragedy had been transformed by the
Christian hope of resurrection and the Christian comic vision of history.

My main argument—that there is a fundamental connection between trinitarian theology and Christian eschatology—was articulated in its essential features by Basil the Great, who pointed out in
his treatise *On the Holy Spirit* (section 47) that the superiority of the
Last Adam to the First Adam has crucial implications for theology
proper. Responding to opponents who argued that a "Second Person" of the Trinity was necessarily an inferior supplement to a "First
Person," Basil writes, "If the second is [always] subordinate to the first,
and since what is subordinate is always inferior to that to which it is
subordinated, according to you, then, the spiritual is inferior to the
physical, and the man from heaven is inferior to the man of dust!"

A disclaimer is necessary before closing this introduction. Despite
the footnotes and other scholarly paraphernalia, this is more an im-
pressionistic essay than an academic treatise. I am confident of the
broad strokes of the thesis, but a great deal more research would be
required to develop it fully, and a fully investigation of these themes
might nuance the argument into quite different directions. *Deep Comedy*, further, operates throughout at a high level of rarified abstrac-
tion, a weakness that might have been corrected by incorporating
anthropological and sociological evidence (on, say, Christian burial
customs). Yet, I had to stop and start somewhere, and I am hopeful

that the thesis is clear enough and plausible enough that it will in-
spire writers with more time and competence to follow up its sug-
gestions.

I
Tragic History

1
Golden Age Past

FOR GREEKS and many other ancient peoples, history was essentially tragic. Things had begun well in a world of plenty and joy, but the world was bound to degenerate and decline until it sputtered and whimpered to a halt. For some, history was seen as a turning wheel, so that the pathetic end was a prelude to a new beginning. Cyclical views of history such as these look more optimistic, but that is only apparent. If it is cyclical, history merely repeats the story of decline again and again, unto ages of ages, the tragedy becoming more banal with each repetition. My argument in this chapter is that the ancient world, and the classical world in particular, knew nothing of eschatology—"eschatology" meaning the view that history moves toward an end that is greater than the beginning. The classical world knew nothing of "deep comedy."

I.

The classical form of the degenerative myth is the myth of the five (or four) metallic ages found in Hesiod. In *Works and Days*, Hesiod reviews history as a regression from the age of gold, through the age of silver, to an age of bronze. The sequence of metallic ages is interrupted by an age of heroes, but then resumes in the fifth age, the age of iron, in which Hesiod unfortunately found himself. The contrast between the two end points of this sequence is particularly striking:

The race of men that the immortals who dwell on Olympus made was first of all of gold. They were in the time of Kronos, when he was king in heaven; and they lived like gods, with carefree heart, remote from toil and misery. Wretched old age did not affect them either, but with hands and feet ever unchanged they enjoyed themselves in feasting, beyond all ills, and they died as if overcome by sleep. All good things were theirs, and the grain-giving soil bore its fruit of its own accord in unstinted plenty, while they at their leisure harvested their fields in contentment amid abundance. Since the earth covered up that race, they have been divine spirits by great Zeus' design, good spirits on the face of the earth, watchers over mortal men, bestowers of wealth: such is the kingly honour that they receive.[1]

The iron race is quite different: "Now it is a race of iron; and they will never cease from toil and misery by day or night, in constant distress, and the gods will give them harsh troubles. Nevertheless, even they shall have good mixed with ill." Before it is all done, the iron age will degenerate into social and political chaos:

Zeus will destroy this race of men also, when at birth they turn out grey at the temples. Nor will father be like children or children to father, nor guest to host or comrade to comrade, nor will a brother be friendly as in former times. Soon they will cease to respect their ageing parents, and will rail at them with harsh words, the ruffians, in ignorance of the gods' punishment; nor are they likely to repay their ageing parents for their nurture. First-law men; one will sack another's town, and there will be no thanks for the man who abides by his oath or for the righteous or worthy man, but instead they will honour the miscreant and the criminal. Law and decency will be in fists.

Hesiod continues in this vein for several more lines, before concluding abruptly by saying that "these grim woes will remain for mortal men, and there will be no help against evil."[2]

---

[1] Hesiod, *Works and Days*, trans. M. L. West, Oxford World's Classics (Oxford: Oxford Univ. Press, 1988), 40.

[2] Ibid., 42.

Several commentators suggest that the myth should be read as something other than a pure myth of degeneration. The metals that characterize the ages get less valuable as the sequence progresses, but at the same time they get more useful and tougher. Besides, Hesiod ends the whole with the lament, "Would that I were not then among the fifth men, but either dead earlier or born later!"[3] which suggests that Hesiod expected the degeneration of the iron age to issue in a renewal, leading ultimately to a renewed golden age. M. L. West has responded to this line of argument by suggesting that "the system as [Hesiod] expounds it is finite and complete; . . . if the logos [word] had had a hopeful ending he would surely have not omitted to mention it." Though Hesiod may personally hope for a renewed age, "it is not necessarily the case that Hesiod's inner convictions coincide with the myth he is telling."[4]

West's comment is sensible, and cyclical interpretations necessarily extrapolate beyond the myth as Hesiod gives it. Yet, even if Hesiod is assuming a cyclical view of history, the larger argument of this chapter would stand, since this myth gives no hope for a movement toward an eschatological "golden age" that would never end. For Hesiod, every golden age, however many there may be, will eventually degenerate into a silver age, and thence to a bronze age, and so on. Thus, in Jean-Pierre Vernant's cyclical reading, each cycle in itself traces a decline. Responding to criticisms of J. Defradas, he writes that "my view was that the sequence of the races made up a complete cycle of decline. Starting off with an age of gold where youth, justice, mutual friendship, and happiness reign, all in their pure state, we end with an age which is its opposite in every respect: it is entirely given over to old age, injustice, quarrelsomeness, and unhappiness."[5]

For different reasons, Robert Nisbet argues that the myth is not properly a "myth of degeneration," since the bronze age is "markedly

---

[3] Ibid., 42.

[4] *Works and Days*, ed. by M. L. West (Oxford: Clarendon Press, 1978), 197.

[5] *Myth and Thought Among the Greeks* (London: Routledge & Kegan Paul, 1983), 39.

better than its silver predecessor, and the next succeeding race, that
of 'hero-men,' is better yet." Further, the iron race is not "as monolith-
ically evil as conventional interpretation would have it."[6] Nisbet is
correct that Hesiod explicitly describes the heroes as superior to the
bronze men, and also right that the iron men are mixed of good and
evil. His claim that the overall trajectory of Hesiod's myth is not degenerative cannot, however, be sustained. The antithesis between the
golden and iron races is too precise and acute to be anything but the
framework of a decline.

In the classical world, in any case, Hesiod's myth was understood
as degenerative. Hesiod's basic framework was taken up by Ovid,
who tells the story in four ages, apparently to bring out the corre-
spondence with the four seasons. Again, the contrast between the
golden and iron ages is striking:

> The Golden Age was first, a time that cherished
> Of its own will, justice and right; no law,
> No punishment, was called for; fearfulness
> Was quite unknown, and the bronze tablets held
> No legal threatening; no suppliant throng
> Studied a judge's face; there were no judges,
> There did not need to be. Trees had not yet
> Been cut and hollowed out, to visit other shores.
> Men were content at home, and had no towns
> With moats and walls around them; and no trumpets
> Blared out alarums; things like swords and helmets
> Had not been heard of. No one needed soldiers.
> People were unaggressive, and unanxious;
> The years went by in peace. And Earth, untroubled,
> Unharried by hoe or plowshare, brought forth all
> That men had need for, and those men were happy,
> Gathering berries from the mountain sides,
> Cherries, or blackcaps, and the edible acorns.

[6] *History of the Idea of Progress* (New York: Basic Books, 1980), 16–17. Vernant makes the
same argument concerning the age of heroes (*Myth and Thought*, 39–40).

Spring was forever, with a west wind blowing
Softly across the flowers no man had planted,
And Earth, unplowed, brought forth rich grain; the field,
Unfallowed, whitened with wheat, and there were rivers
Of milk, and rivers of honey, and golden nectar
Dripped from the dark-green oak-trees.[7]

Strikingly, for Ovid even more than for Hesiod, men of the golden age were completely innocent of culture, including agri-culture, as well as of social and political institutions and of economic activities. For both, culture is a product of the process of degeneration, a "fall" from nature. Though both would no doubt endorse this as a "fortunate fall," culture remains a product of the tragedy of human history. We will meet this notion that culture is a contaminating supplement to an originally pure nature again and again in both ancient and modern writers.

As in Hesiod, the iron age differs from the golden at nearly every point:

The Iron Age succeeded, whose base vein
Let loose all evil: modesty and truth
And righteousness fled earth, and in their place
Came trickery and slyness, plotting, swindling,
Violence and the damned desire of having.
Men spread their sails to winds unknown to sailors,
The pines came down their mountain-sides, to revel
And leap in the deep waters, and the ground,
Free, once, to everyone, like air and sunshine,
Was stepped off by surveyors. The rich earth,
Good giver of all the bounty of the harvest,
Was asked for more; they dug into her vitals,
Pried out the wealth a kinder lord had hidden
In Stygian shadow, all that precious metal,
The root of evil. They found the guilt of iron,

---

[7] Trans. Rolfe Humphries (Bloomington, Ind.: Indiana Univ. Press, 1960), 5–6.

And gold, more guilty still. And War came forth
That uses both to fight with; bloody hands
Brandished the clashing weapons. Men lived on plunder.
Guest was not safe from host, nor brother from brother,
A man would kill his wife, a wife her husband,
Stepmothers, dire and dreadful, stirred their brews
With poisonous aconite, and sons would hustle
Fathers to death, and Piety lay vanquished,
And the maiden Justice, last of all immortals,
Fled from blood earth.

Even heaven is not peaceful during the iron age: giants attacked the
dwellings of the gods, and when Zeus struck them dead to earth with
a thunderbolt, their blood impregnated Earth so that she produced
new men, "sons of blood," who were "contemptuous of the gods, and
murder-hungry and violent."[8] Zeus arrested the decline by sending
a great flood that wiped the slate clean. Even if Ovid did not believe
the cycle of metals would return, it is clear he presented the early
life of man as a decline. And, given that Ovid viewed reality as permanent flux, he therefore gives little hope that Zeus's victory is permanent.

Juvenal, likewise, understood the myth as a description of decline,
though one that was insufficient to account for the corruption of his
own first-century A.D. situation:

A ninth age is in motion, a period worse than the times
Of iron, for whose viciousness has Nature herself
Not found a name to impose after any metal.[9]

Greek poets such as Theognis of Megara, Empedocles, and Aratus,
and Roman poets like Lucretius and Catullus, all make more or less

---

[8] Ibid, 7.

[9] Satire 13.28–30 in Juvenal, *Sixteen Satires Upon the Ancient Harlot*, trans. Steven Robinson
(Manchester: Carcanet New Press, 1983), 179. Variations of the four/five age scheme,
correlated to metals, appear in Sumerian, Babylonian, Zoroastrian, and Indian mytholo-
gies (cf. West's notes in the Oxford edition of *Works and Days*, 174–177).

explicit use of the metallic myth and treat it as a myth of degenera-
tion.[10] The age of sons is always worse than the age of the fathers,
and the more distant the fathers the more superior they are. E. R.
Dodds summarizes the situation of the ancient world as follows:
"Later poets [than Hesiod] who saw history in cyclic terms tended
to follow Hesiod's example: they have much to say about the Lost
Paradise, but almost nothing, until Virgil, about Paradise Regained.
The cyclic theory is most often found in the service of pessimism."[11]
The last state is always worse than the first.

II.

There are, to be sure, occasional affirmations of a conception of
progress in Greco-Roman literature that could be taken as hints and
gestures toward an eschatological conception of history. Xenophanes
said that the gods did not reveal everything to mankind at the beginning, but "in the course of time by research men discover improve-
ments."[12] Aeschylus gave a more elaborate statement of human
achievement and progress to Prometheus:

> listen to the tale
Of human sufferings, and how at first
Senseless as beasts I gave men sense, possessed them
Of mind. I speak not in contempt of man;
I do but tell of good gifts I conferred.
In the beginning, seeing they saw amiss,
And hearing heard not, but, like phantoms huddled
In dreams, the perplexed story of their days
Confounded; knowing neither timber-work
Nor brick-built dwellings basking in the light,
But dug for themselves holes, wherein like ants,
That hardly may contend against a breath,

[10] For details, see Patricia A. Johnston, *Vergil's Agricultural Golden Age: A Study of the Georgics* (Leiden: Brill, 1980), 15–40.
[11] E. R. Dodds, *The Ancient Concept of Progress and Other Essays on Greek Literature and Beliefs* (Oxford: Clarendon, 1973), 4.
[12] Ibid., 4.

They dwelt in burrows of their unsunned caves. . . .
               utterly without knowledge
Moiled, until I the rising of the stars
Showed them, and when they set, though much obscure.
Moreover, number, the most excellent
Of all inventions, I for them devised,
And gave them writing that retaineth all,
The serviceable mother of the Muse.
I was the first that yoked unmanageable beasts,
To serve as slaves with collar and with pack.
And take upon themselves, to man's relief,
The heaviest labour of his hands: and I
Tamed to the rein and drove in wheeled cars
The horse, of sumptuous pride the ornament.
And those sea-wanderers with the wings of cloth,
The shipman's wagons, none but I contrived.
These manifold inventions for mankind
I perfected.[13]

A choral ode from Sophocles' *Antigone* makes similar claims:

Wonders are many, and none is more wonderful than man; the power
that crosses the white sea, driven by the stormy south-wind, making a path under surges that threaten to engulf him; and Earth, the
eldest of the gods, the immortal, the unwearied, doth he wear, turning the soil with the offspring of horses, as the ploughs go to and
fro from year to year. . . .

   And speech, and wind-swift of thought, and all the moods that
mould a state, hath he taught himself; and how to flee the arrows of
the frost, when 'tis hard lodging under the clear sky, and the arrows
of the rushing rain; yea, he hath resources for all; without resource
he meets nothing that must come: only against Death shall he call
for aid in vain; but from baffling maladies he had devised escapes.[14]

---

[13] Aeschylus, *Prometheus Bound*, trans. G. M. Cookson, in vol. 5 of Great Books of the
Western World (Chicago: Encyclopedia Britannica, 1952), 44–45. See Dodds, *Ancient
Concept*, 5–6, for a discussion of this passage.
   [14] Sophocles, *Antigone*, trans. Richard C. Jebb, in vol. 5 of Great Books of the Western
World (Chicago: Encyclopedia Britannica, 1952), 134.

As Dodds points out, this passage appears to say more than it does. The cleverness that the chorus celebrates here is not an undiluted good: "Cunning beyond fancy's dream is the fertile skill which brings him, now to evil, now to good." Sophocles, further, hardly presents a hopeful portrait of life in the overall scheme of the *Oedipus* cycle. Such expressions of a hope for human progress appear mainly in fifth-century Athens, but this is an exceptional period in this regard throughout ancient history. He adds, more generally, that while "it is untrue that the idea of progress was wholly foreign to Antiquity," still "our evidence suggests that only during a limited period in the fifth century was it widely accepted by the educated public at large."[15]

Virgil was the first to state an explicit belief in a restored golden age and also the first to claim that the dawning of the new age was imminent.[16] In his Fourth Eclogue (the so-called "Messianic Eclogue"), Virgil wrote of the birth of a child through whom the new golden age would be born. Initially, while the child is still young, the golden age will come only in part, but as the child grows and reaches manhood, the golden age will dawn in earnest. When, like a latter-day Hercules, he assumes full humanity, not only war but commerce and farming will cease, because the earth will be as fruitful as it was in the long-ago days of the original golden age:

> when the years have confirmed you in full manhood,
> Traders will retire from the sea, from the pine-built vessels
> They used for commerce: every land will be self-supporting.
> The soil will need no harrowing, the vine no pruning-knife;
> And the tough ploughman may at least unyoke his oxen.
> We shall stop treating wool with artificial dyes,
> For the ram himself in his pasture will change his fleece's colour,

---

[15] *Ancient Concept*, 24.

[16] Ibid., 21. Johnston, in *Vergil's Agricultural Golden Age*, claims that "One of the crucial distinctions between Vergil's conception of a golden age and that of his predecessors is the fact that Vergil's golden age can recur" (8).

Now to a charming purple, now to a saffron hue,
And grazing lambs will dress themselves in coats of scarlet.[17]

Wendell Clausen nicely summarizes this portion of the Eclogue:
"During this period of military expansion in the eastern Mediterra-
nean and beyond, the Golden Age will insensibly be merged, as the
boy grows to manhood, with the age of heroes; like the golden, in
Hesiod, an age of preternatural felicity, but, unlike the golden, im-
mune to deterioration."[18] Virgil's celebration of the peace brought
by the Augustan empire in the *Aeneid* rings the changes on similar
themes, as does Horace's celebration of restored Roman virtue in the
Carmen Saeculare. In a somewhat similar vein, Horace's Sixteenth
Epode describes the "Blessed Fields and Wealthy Isles" where the
golden age continues into the present. Those islands are lands of fruitfulness, but not of cultivation:

where every year the land unploughed gives grain,
and vines unpruned are never out of flower,
and olive shoots unfailing bud and set their fruit,
and dusky fig ungrafted graces its own tree."[19]

Virgil comes closer than any in the classical world came to a conception of an eschatological resolution to history. But two observations will indicate the distance between Virgil and the Christian
eschatology that will be described in the next chapter. First, Virgil's
renewed golden age is literally a return to the origin, not a supplement or advance from the origin. All cultural supplements to nature
are to be removed in the golden age, since, like Ovid, he believes that

---

[17] Virgil, *The Eclogues of Virgil*, trans. C. Day Lewis (London: Jonathan Cape, 1963), 24.
For a concise overview of this poem and its Christian use, see Wendell Clausen's "Com-
mentary" in *Virgil: Eclogues*, Latin text with introduction and commentary by Clausen
(Oxford: Clarendon, 1994), 119–130.

[18] Clausen, "Commentary," 125.

[19] Horace, *Complete Odes and Epodes*, trans. David West, Oxford World's Classics (Oxford: Oxford Univ. Press, 1997), 18–20.

all these cultural supplementations are aspects of a "fall" from natural bliss. Virgil does not imagine a garden-city or even a literal return to Eden, but a world scoured of commerce, agriculture, labor, travel and trade. Second, Virgil's apparent optimism in the Fourth Eclogue and elsewhere is crossed by his persistent melodramatic sentimentalism. Aeneas establishes a purported *imperium sine fine*, but does so through tears and laments, so that Aeneas's *sunt lacrimae rerum* ("here are the tears of things" or "here they weep for how the world goes"), uttered as he examines the depictions of the Trojan War on the walls of Juno's temple in Carthage, is something of a Virgilian motto. Virgil is nowhere more himself than when he is wringing his readers' hearts with a pathetic description of the death of a beautiful youth (Marcellus in *Aeneid* Book 6, and Pallas in Book 9).

It also appears that Virgil's enthusiasm was checked by later events. The older and presumably wiser Virgil of the *Georgics* recognized that the golden age had not materialized, that there was no going back to the age before the age of Jupiter, and that tilling the soil remained the arduous price of survival:

> The first rule in farming
> Is that you are never to hope for an easy way.
> The land demands your effort. Body and mind
> Are sharpened, that undisturbed would grow vague with sloth.
> Before Jupiter's reign the fields had no masters.
> Even to mark out land and divide it with bounds
> Was unlawful. No one took thought of yours or mine
> While the generous earth gave enough for every need.
> Jupiter first put the poison in black snakes
> Sent wolves marauding, set the clam sea heaving,
> Shook honey off the leaves, took fire away,
> And stopped the wine that ran everywhere in streams.[20]

---

[20] Georgic 1 in Virgil, *The Georgics*, trans. Robert Wells (Manchester: Carcanet New Press, 1982), 32–33.

Richard Thomas comments,

> The passage places the cultural setting of the *Georgics* after the Fall,
> and it is a passage which Virgil intends the reader to apply through-
> out the poem; where the language of the golden age is found, it ei-
> ther creates a conflict with the realities of the poem (2.136–76,
> 458–540nn.), or it is applied with irony (3.537–45n.). The agents
> of Jupiter are toil and want, toil which is insatiable and pervasive,
> and want which presses when times are hard.[21]

Patricia Johnston argues, on the contrary, that Jupiter's imposition
of labor and want is for the good of men, since freedom from work
led to "dulled wits and lethargy." In the *Georgics*, on her reading, Virgil
renounces the metallic myth as he told it in the *Eclogues* and subverts
the traditional meanings of the metals, but this does not lead to de-
spairing nostalgia. Instead, the farmer's life is itself a kind of golden
age. The golden age is no longer an age *before* cultivation but is transformed into the age of agrarian simplicity, one that the farmer can
help to usher in by diligent labor.[22] Johnston's is an interesting and
perhaps correct thesis, but even on her reading the golden age of the
Georgics is profoundly chastened. Virgil's conception of history is certainly not, on any reading, "deeply comic."

But to see that, I need to give a fuller exposition of "deep comedy." That is the subject of chapter 2.

---

[21] *Virgil: Georgics*, 2 vols. (Cambridge: Cambridge Univ. Press, 1988), 1:17. Thomas's pessimistic reading of the Georgics has been challenged by Llewlyn Morgan in *Patterns of Redemption in Virgil's Georgics* (Cambridge: Cambridge Univ. Press, 1999).

[22] *Vergil's Agricultural Golden Age*, 47–61.

2

The Best Is Yet to Be

ANCIENT WISDOM was tragic wisdom. It was the wisdom of the Stoic who had learned not to expect too much, who had adjusted himself to the grim realities of Murphy's Law, who realized that history, like the individual's life, was a sometimes slow, sometimes rapid but always inexorable progress toward death. Wisdom involved disciplining, chastening, and controlling hope, if not its surgical removal. Hope was a youthful and charming thing, but had to give way to the grim realism of age. "A joyful sage": it is an impossible description by ancient standards.

Against the classical nostalgia for a golden age lost and unlikely to be revived, the Bible, beginning with the prophets of Israel and continuing into the New Testament, holds out the promise of a future age of glory, peace, justice, and abundance. The last state is not worse than the first. In every way, the last state is superior to the first, and infinitely superior to the painful evils of the ages between first and last.

I.

The main biblical passage that (perhaps) alludes to the Hesiodic myth of the declining and degenerating metallic ages is Daniel 2, and there the myth is radically subverted. In a dream, Nebuchadnezzar sees a statue consisting of a head of gold, a torso of silver, thighs of bronze, legs of iron, and feet of iron mixed with clay being struck by a stone "cut out without hands," which crushes the statue to powder (Daniel 2:31–35). Once the stone has demolished the composite statue, it "became a great mountain and filled the whole earth" (v. 35). Daniel interprets this as a vision of the coming of the kingdom of the "God of heaven" that "will crush and put an end to all these kingdoms, but it will itself endure forever" (v. 45). Even if the vision is somehow alluding to the Hesiodic myth, which is doubtful, the vision ends with a new, greater, and everlasting kingdom, challenging both the cyclical and the degenerative readings of Hesiod.

Isaiah's prophecies have a similar shape. Instead of looking back in regret to a lost Davidic kingdom and the tarnished glories of Solomon, Isaiah is full of the promise of a future "golden age," when the lion will lie down with the lamb (11:1–10), when the mountain of the house of the Lord will be established as chief of the mountains and become a place of pilgrimage for the Gentiles (2:2–4), when the glory of Yahweh will be revealed to the nations (40:5), proving all idols to be nothing and less than nothing. Rather than look back to the exodus from Egypt, Isaiah prophesies that Yahweh is going to act with such power and splendor that Israel herself will forget her founding event (43:14–21). Isaiah's visions, to be sure, are structured by Israel's past. Hope is placed in a new David (a "Branch from Jesse"), and redemption from Babylon is imagined as a new exodus and a new conquest. But the keynote is *not* cyclical, as if Israel were simply going to go through the same thing all over again. The keynote of the prophecy is Yahweh's declaration that, "Behold, I do something new" (43:19; cf. 42:9; 48:6). Isaiah's repeated emphasis on the fact that the Creator-God Yahweh is doing the "new thing" suggests that only a doctrine of creation, with its implied eschatology, can provide theological ground for real newness and invention. Unless the world comes from an inexhaustibly infinite Creator, there is always going to be some limit on where human history can go. Since God is truly infinite, there is no bar to infinite progression of the new. History will "end" with man still facing infinite horizons yet to achieve— which is to say, it will not end. There will be a judgment and a resurrection, but that will be the first moment of a new phase of human development and emphatically *not* an entry into a static existence.

Late in his prophecy, Isaiah employs the metallic imagery of Daniel 2, and his use of the imagery runs counter to Hesiod. Speaking words of comfort to Jerusalem and Judah, Isaiah writes,

> Whereas you have been forsaken and hated with no one passing through, I will make you an everlasting pride, a joy from generation to generation. You will also suck the milk of nations, and will suck the breast of kings; then you will know that I, Yahweh, am your Savior, and your Redeemer, the Mighty One of Jacob. Instead of bronze I will bring gold, and instead of iron I will bring silver, and instead of wood, bronze, and instead of stones, iron. And I will make peace your administrators, and righteousness your overseers. (Is. 60:15–17)

This reversal of Judah's fortunes and the restoration of a prior "golden age" will see the end of violence from enemies (v. 18), an eternal sun (v. 19), and fruitfulness and prosperity on all sides. Ezekiel's prophecy begins with Yahweh's abandonment of the temple (Ezek. 8–11), moves through a series of severe judgments toward return and resurrection (chaps. 36–37) and the construction of an awe-inspiring temple-city that is superior in every respect to the temple that is destroyed at the outset of the chapter (chaps. 40–48).[1]

Jeremiah is worth lingering over for a few moments, for no other prophet in Scripture is so full of tears as the "weeping prophet." As the personification of the remnant and the suffering servant Israel, Jeremiah experiences intense anguish at the fall of Jerusalem. Few passages of ancient literature can equal the sense of desolation in the opening verses of Lamentations:

> How lonely sits the city
> That was full of people.

---

[1] For a more detailed discussion of this narrative flow, see my *A House for My Name: A Survey of the Old Testament* (Moscow, Idaho: Canon, 2000), 215–222.

> She has become like a widow
> Who was once great among the nations.
> She who was a princess among the provinces
> Has become a forced laborer. (Lam. 1:1)

Even Yahweh Himself joins in the grief, so that in some passages it is impossible to tell whether Yahweh or Jeremiah is speaking:

> "Shall I not punish them for these things?" declares Yahweh. "On a nation such as this, shall I not avenge Myself? For the mountains I will take up a weeping and wailing, and for the pastures of the wilderness a dirge, because they are laid waste, so that no one passes through, and the lowing of the cattle is not heard; both the birds of the sky and the beasts have fled; they are gone. And I will make Jerusalem a heap of ruins, a haunt of jackals; and I will make the cities of Judah a desolation, without inhabitant." (Jer. 9:9–11)

> "And I will make an end of Moab," declares Yahweh, "the one who offers sacrifice on the high place and the one who burns incense to his gods. Therefore my heart wails for Moab like flutes; My heart also wails like flutes for the men of Kir-heres." (Jeremiah 48:35–36)

Perhaps here we have an example of a "tragic" conception of Israel's future.

At the center of Jeremiah's prophecy, however, is the promise of a new and better covenant (Jeremiah 31:27–38),[2] which Jeremiah announces with several repetitions of the phrase "days are coming" (31:27, 31, 38). This promised restoration reverses, systematically and completely, the desolations described in passages such as Jeremiah 9. Pastures that had been laid waste will be restored (31:23–24), the land that was without inhabitant will be resown (31:27), all that has been thrown down will be rebuilt, what has been uprooted will be

---

[2] For a structural analysis showing that chapters 30–33 form the chiastic center of Jeremiah's prophecy, see David A. Dorsey, *The Literary Structure of the Old Testament: A Commentary on Genesis–Malachi* (Grand Rapids: Baker, 1999), 236–245.

replanted, and what has been overthrown will be set straight (31:28). Even the anguish of the prophet feeds off of hope. What gives Jeremiah's lamentations their passion is the recognition that it did not have to turn out this way. Israel had all blessings and all hope, and wasted it: "Has a nation changed gods, when they were not gods? But My people have changed their glory for that which does not profit." Heaven shudders because "My people have committed two errors: They have forsaken Me, the fountain of living waters, to hew for themselves cisterns, broken cisterns, that can hold no water" (2:11–13). Yahweh and His prophet weep over Israel because Israel could have enjoyed abundant life and turned away. The problem is not that history inevitably declines toward catastrophe. The problem is simply that Israel willfully sinned and refused repentance. In Jeremiah, comic possibility shines a light that deepens the shadows of disaster. The situation is similar in Job, whose perplexity at suffering is proportionate to his confidence that Yahweh is just and all-powerful.

Ecclesiastes provides the closest analogy in the Old Testament to ancient "tragic wisdom." It is often interpreted as if Solomon were promoting a pessimistic and skeptical view of life. In part, these interpretations are grounded in a mistranslation of the key Hebrew word *hebel* (Ecclesiastes 1:1–2 and throughout). Its basic meaning is "vapor" but the word is translated as "vanity" or even "meaningless" in most English Bibles. "Vapor" is much more suitable. What Solomon explores in the book is the brevity and "vaporousness" of life. Because everything shifts and changes (3:1–8), because the world is full of unexplained paradoxes like the ever-filling but never-full sea (1:7), because everyone's life, whether king or slave, ends in death (2:16). Trying to shape the world is like trying to sculpt figures from mist.[3] Faced with such a world, the dead are to be congratulated more than the living for escaping the incessant repetitions of life, and "better off than both of them is the one who has never existed, who has never seen the evil activity that is done under the sun" (4:2–3).

---

[3] This image is from James B. Jordan's taped lectures on Daniel, available from Biblical Horizons (P.O. Box 1096, Niceville, FL 32588).

The various efforts to reconcile Ecclesiastes with the "orthodoxy" of the Hebrew Bible are legion, and most are useless or worse. The idea, promoted by some evangelical scholars, that there are "two voices" at work in the book—one orthodox and the other skeptical and pessimistic—is a counsel of despair. The problem with these efforts is that they fail to recognize the profound "orthodoxy" of Ecclesiastes itself. Like the closing chapters of Job, Ecclesiastes teaches that there is more in heaven and earth than is dreamed of in our philosophies or theologies, that God is up to more than we can possibly conceive, and that, limited and finite as we are, it is only natural that our grasp of the pattern of history is partial and our control of life is limited.

The distance between tragic wisdom and the wisdom of Solomon could hardly be greater. Where ancient tragic wisdom reasons from the contradictions and fluxes of life toward a sense of resignation, Solomon reasons from the changes and fluxes and contradictions of life toward joy:

There is nothing better for a man than to eat and drink and tell himself that his labor is good. This also I have seen, that it is from the hand of God. (2:24)

I know that there is nothing better for them than to rejoice and to do good in one's lifetime; moreover, that every man who eats and drinks sees good in all his labor—it is the gift of God. (3:12–13)

And I have seen that nothing is better than that man should be happy in his activities, for that is his lot. For who will bring him to see what will occur after him? (3:22)

Here is what I have seen to be good and fitting: to eat, to drink and enjoy oneself in all one's labor in which he toils under the sun during the years of his life which God has given him; for this is his reward. (5:18)

Enjoy life with the woman whom you love all the days of your life
of vapor which He has given to you under the sun; for this is your
reward in life, and in your toil in which you have labored under the
sun. (9:7)

In each of these passages, the exhortation to joy, feasting, and pro-
ductive labor is *inferred from* the fact that life is vaporous and short.
Joy is not a contradiction to the reality of a vaporous world; joy is
the "fitting" response to a vaporous world. This is neither Stoic resignation nor Epicurean hedonism. Epicurean "joy" is a desperate whis-
tling past the graveyard, a hedonism haunted by the realization that
the world is under no one's control. Epicurean joy is finally tragic
joy. Solomonic joy is a hedonism that arises from the confidence that
the world is always under Yahweh's control. Solomon is saying that
the world itself teaches us that it is not under our control, but
Solomon adds the implication that the world is under God's control.
Instead of chafing at our finitude and yearning to be as gods, Solomon
counsels that we rejoice in our limits and in all the vaporous life that
we are given.

The New Testament turns the perspective of the Hebrew prophets into a framework for the whole of human history. As noted above,
this "comic" story provides the overall frame for the Christian Bible,
which begins with the garden of Eden and ends with a city that is a
glorification or enhancement of the original setting. Like Eden, the
New Jerusalem is a well-watered place (Rev. 22:2; cf. Gen. 2:10–
11; 13:10). Instead of a single tree of life in the midst of the garden
(Gen. 2:9), the New Jerusalem's river is lined with trees of life, "bear-
ing twelve fruit, yielding fruit every month; and the leaves were for
the healing of the nations" (Rev. 22:2). The alternation of night and
day that was determined on the first day of the creation week (Gen.
1:3–5) is replaced by an eternal day in which "there shall no longer
be night." The sun, created on the fourth day (Gen. 1:14–19), will
be replaced by the direct radiance of the uncreated light of God:
"They shall not have need of the light of a lamp nor of the sun, be-

cause the Lord God will illumine them" (Rev. 22:5).[4] Like the days of creation, which move from evening to morning, biblical history moves from darkness to light, from the darkness, emptiness, and formlessness of the original creation (Gen. 1:2) to the lighted and teeming city of Revelation. History moves toward day. Jesus' first "sign" in John's gospel (2:1–11) is a symbolic announcement of the same reality. The wedding guests are perfect classicists, who think that things must get worse as time passes. Reversing common practice, Jesus gives better wine at the end of the feast than He gave at the beginning. The later is better.

A basic structure of Pauline theology—the contrast of first and last ($\varepsilon\sigma\chi\alpha\tau\sigma\varsigma$) Adams—makes the same point (Rom. 5:12–21; 1 Cor. 15:45). In Romans 5, Paul summarizes human history by reference to its two leading men. By the first man, Adam, sin entered the world and death through sin, but through the second man, the Last Adam, the reign of sin and death has been replaced by the reign of life in those who have received the gift of grace and righteousness (5:14, 17). From Adam to Jesus, death reigned, but with Jesus' resurrection life has entered the world. Ultimately, that reign of life will engulf the entire creation. Though it was subjected to futility, creation will be "set free from its slavery to corruption into the freedom of the glory of the sons of God." Though it now "groans and suffers the pains of childbirth," it will one day come to delivery when the day arrives for our "adoption as sons," the "redemption of the body" (Rom. 8:18–25).

Elsewhere, Paul describes the same historical movement in other terms. In 2 Corinthians 3, he compares his own ministry as a steward of the New Covenant to the stewardship of Moses in the Old. The contrast is played out in several different registers:

---

[4] For more extended reflections on the literary and theological connections between Genesis 1–2 and Revelation 21–22, see William J. Dumbrell, *The End of the Beginnings: Revelation 21–22 and the Old Testament,* Moore Theological College Lecture Series (Homebush West, Australia: Lancer, 1985), chapter 5.

Old	New
Letter	Spirit
Tablets of stone	Tablets of human hearts
Kills	Gives life
Ministry of condemnation	Ministry of righteousness
Glory	Surpassing glory
Veil	Veil removed
Minds hardened	(Minds softened)
(Slavery)	Liberty

At every point, the New Covenant is superior, though later. Nor is progress limited to the once-for-all transition from the Old to New. Paul expects a continuing expansion of glory, a continuous glorification of the more glorious, the surpassingly glorious, new covenant: "We all, with unveiled face, beholding as in a mirror the glory of the Lord, are being transformed into the same image from glory to glory, just as from the Lord, the Spirit" (3:18).

The gospel story itself, centrally a story of humiliation giving way to glorification, is the most obvious source for the comic vision of the New Testament. For Jesus, death is not the final word, and the latter state for Jesus is better than the first, for by the resurrection Jesus enters into the life of the age to come, the immortality, power, glory of a spiritual body. The resurrection of Jesus means the inbreaking of eschatological life, the life of the resurrection, into the present. Through the gift of the Spirit at Pentecost, dependent on the resurrection and ascension of the Son, the life of the end is already offered, given, received. Pentecost means the restoration of all things, and marks the beginning of a progress toward a *future* golden age. Throughout the Old Testament prophetic books, the promise of the Spirit is linked with the restoration of humanity and the entire creation.

For the land of my people in which thorns and briars shall come up;
Yea for all the joyful houses, and for the jubilant city.
Because the palace has been abandoned, the populated city forsaken.

Hill and watchtower have become caves forever,
A delight for wild donkeys, a pasture for flocks;
Until the Spirit is poured out upon us from on high,
And the wilderness becomes a fertile field
And the fertile field is considered a forest.
Then justice will dwell in the wilderness,
And righteousness will abide in the fertile field. (Isaiah 32:13–16)

I will put My Spirit within you and cause you to walk in My stat-
utes, and you will be careful to observe My ordinances. You will live
in the land that I gave to your forefathers; so you will be My people,
and I will be your God. . . . I will multiply the fruit of the tree and
the produce of the field, so that you will not receive again the dis-
grace of famine among the nations. . . . On the day that I cleanse
you from all your iniquities, I will cause the cities to be inhabited,
and the waste places will be rebuilt. The desolate land will be culti-
vated instead of being a desolation in the sight of everyone who
passes by. They will say, "This desolate land has become like the garden of Eden; and the waste, desolate and ruined cities are fortified
and inhabited." (Ezek. 36:27–28, 30, 33–35)

At Pentecost, a splintered and fragmented humanity was reunited
through a miracle of language, reversing the curse of Babel. Through
the Spirit, the resurrection power of Jesus heals not only broken men,
but broken nations and a broken world.

At the same time, the gospel narratives, because they include the
ineradicable moments of betrayal, torture, injustice, and cross, prevent the Christian understanding of history from becoming trivially
comic or sentimental. Resurrection does indeed follow the cross and
swallows up the sorrow in astonished surprise and joy, but, as David
Bentley Hart has argued, the light of the resurrection intensifies the
pain of death by destroying the comforting illusions of ancient resignation. The pattern of Jeremiah's prophecy is the pattern of the gospel narratives; resurrection "opens up another, still deeper kind of
pain: it requires of faith something even more terrible than submis-
sion before the violence of being and acceptance of fate," thus throw-

ing the believer "out upon the turbid seas of boundless hope and boundless hunger." Because the resurrection vindicates the Crucified, not the crucifixion, the gospel story undercuts any easy moralism or sentimental liberalism.[5] Yet, though the resurrection opens up possibilities that could not even be imagined by ancient man, it also *promises* the fulfillment of those possibilities. If it provokes unimagined hunger, it also gives hope for unimagined satisfaction. Through its moment of cross and death, the story remains ultimately comic, finally and decisively comic, wildly and insanely comic.

Thus the cross and resurrection intensify sadness and the sense of loss, and in a sense make tragedy more tragic. As Hart explains, for the ancient world, tragedy was not horrifying but comforting, providing the hope of a beautiful, heroic, and noble death. The resurrection exposes the tragic consolations regarding death as hollow, and thus throws the believer on a wild surmise of faith and hope. Resurrection "forbids faith the consolations of tragic wisdom; it places all hope and all consolation upon the insane expectation that what is lost will be given back, not as a heroic wisdom (death has been robbed of its tragic beauty) but as the gift it always was." As Mel Gibson's *Passion* reminds us in bloody detail, death can no longer, after the cross, be glorious and heroic; death is simply death, an enemy, hopeless and meaningless—but for the faith that the loss will be restored. Because of the resurrection (as Hart argued in an article in *First Things*) there is simply no choice but faith in Christ or the *nihil* of meaninglessness—a nihilism that can be pagan celebration or pagan melancholy but is not hope or joy. No noble, no heroic, no tragic compromise position will do, given the fact of the cross. Death must simply be conquered by resurrection. It can no longer provide meaning and dignity.

The gospel entered the world telling a radically new story about man and history, a story that challenged tragic sadness with joy and

---

[5] *The Beauty of the Infinite: The Aesthetics of Christian Truth* (Grand Rapids: Eerdmans, 2003), 392.

hope, and robbed tragic consolations of their healing power. Most especially, the gospel entered the world announcing that death did not reign, but had yielded to the reign of life. Unfortunately, many Christians mentally adjust the astonishing claims of the New Testament and in so doing weaken it beyond recognition. Paul's words, it is thought, must apply to "spiritual" realities or to "salvation history," but not to the actual history of humanity. The reasons for making this adjustment are obvious. Death, after all, continues to reign as much as ever, and sin remains quite popular, as anyone knows who reads a newspaper, flips on the TV news, or attends an Episcopal church. Neither Jesus nor Paul would have had any sympathy for these adjustments. Adam was as historical a person as you or I, and so was Jesus. Death entered a good world because of the transgression of Adam, and new life entered the sinful world through the obedience of Jesus and the Spirit He sent. Adam's sin was an historical event, and so was the resurrection of Jesus and so was Pentecost. These are the key points in a history that includes Abraham, David, Solomon, Nebuchadnezzar, Cyrus the Persian, and Caesar Augustus, not to mention Charlemagne, Napoleon, Saddam Hussein and Osama bin Laden. In Paul's estimation, anyone who thought that the new life through Jesus pertained to some realm outside this history was simply an unbeliever. For the gospel says otherwise.

Certainly, discerning this new life at work in the world is an act of faith, but faith is not irrational or a leap into the dark against evidence. If the gospel is true, if new life was unleashed in the world on Easter morning, then we would expect there to be some signs that this is the case. And, as the church fathers were at pains to point out, we do. Athanasius noted all the pagans turning from their idols, all the warring tribes become brothers, all the swords being beaten to plowshares, and used these things to expound the effects of the Incarnation. Paul, however, means exactly what he says: the coming of Jesus, and particularly the resurrection of Jesus, means that death and sin are themselves doomed, and life is already on the march to conquer death. Darkness is being dispelled because Light has come and the darkness could neither comprehend nor overcome it (John 1:5).

II.

This account of the comic shape of biblical history and the gospel narrative has been challenged by a number of theologians and biblical scholars in recent years. Biblical scholars have attempted to show that the Bible's stories fit into the generic categories of ancient drama or poetry, and have tried to show in particular that certain biblical narratives can be classified as tragedy. In my view, these are not successful efforts either in general or in detailed treatment of texts. In her *Tragedy and Biblical Narrative*, for instance, Cheryl Exum emphasizes the struggle against fate/gods/God as a key element of tragedy:

> Tragic heroes have the *hubris*—sometimes in authentic greatness, sometimes in delusion—to defy the universe, not in a stoic defiance but in an insistence on their moral integrity (justified or not). Because they refuse, they will be broken. . . . It is not that there is "no way out whatsoever," as Jaspers asserts, but that there is no way out without denying oneself. Saul refuses to acquiesce, he will hold on to the kingship at whatever the cost, rejecting the easy way out. There is a "way out" and Saul's son Jonathan, by yielding his right to the throne to David, shows what it is, but at the cost of his identity, which, as we shall see, becomes submerged into David's.[6]

It is true that Saul is tragic in the sense that Exum uses the term, but it is also clear that his tragedy is the result of his own intransigence. The story clearly endorses precisely the "easy way out"—the way of Jonathan, the way of self-denial—which is, of course, the very difficult way out, since it means effacing (but also eventually finding) one's own identity before Yahweh and before the "rival," David. Jonathan, characterized by self-denial and even "discipleship," is

---

[6] J. Cheryl Exum, *Tragedy and Biblical Narrative: Arrows of the Almighty* (Cambridge: Cambridge University Press, 1992), 12.

manifestly the hero of the story.[7] One can say that the Bible presents Saul as "tragic," but only if we are willing to give up calling him, in any sense, a "hero." Again, as in Jeremiah and the gospels, Saul's story leaves one with an intense sense of loss precisely because there *was* a way out, precisely because life was a real option.

Further, Exum emphasizes that the tragic hero struggles particularly to *understand* the fate that brings tragic consequences. Oedipus is a titanic figure because he relentlessly pursues the truth of his situation. Again, the Bible has a "tragic dimension" in the sense that it recognizes the reality of this kind of struggle, yet the Bible does not reckon this as a heroic struggle—a struggle to be commended and supported. The titanic desire and need to know is the desire to be as God, to know as God, the lust to have the complete and finished story as God does. Put differently, it is a refusal of faith, a refusal to trust that God, however random and wild He may appear and be, will do right. It is a refusal to learn the wisdom of Ecclesiastes. From a biblical perspective, the tragic hero is simply a character who refuses to trust that God knows what He's about with His universe, and will accept his "fate" only if he can see all its causes and ramifications. The tragic protagonist longs to live by sight. Job, faced with "tragic" suffering, demands to know the cause. Yahweh appears and answers no questions; the revelation of Yahweh in a whirlwind is sufficient to stop Job's mouth. The tragic pursuit of knowledge is a refusal of Solomonic wisdom as expressed in Ecclesiastes, the wisdom that rejoices in limitation, rejoices precisely because this vaporous world is not under our control.

Finally, Exum seems to imply that tragedy rests on a necessary guilt:

> Tragedy does not clearly distinguish guilt and innocence. Kierkegaard speaks of "authentic tragic guilt in its ambiguous guiltlessness." The heroes of tragedy are innocent in the sense that their misfor-

---

[7] For discussion, which examines Jonathan in Girardian terms as a man who renounces mimetic rivalry, see my *A Son to Me: An Exposition of 1 & 2 Samuel* (Moscow, Idaho: Canon, 2003), 91–93, 106–112.

tune is far greater than anything their deeds have provoked, and guilty both as members of a guilty society and by virtue of living in a world where such injustices simply happen. This is Ricoeur's "guiltiness of being" and Jaspers' "guilt of existence."[8]

Perhaps this is a way of stating a doctrine of original sin, but it appears that Exum means something more. Her "guilt of existence" appears to be a guilt inherent in human existence as such. The Bible denies that there is guilt in human existence as such; sin and consequent guilt *entered* human life, as Paul puts it in Romans 5, and Jesus could live a fully authentic human life "yet without sin." Exum is explicit that the "darkness" of the original creation represents a primal chaos that has to be "controlled and delimited by the deity" and yet remains "potentially threatening remnants of chaos." Thus, "If we seek the origin of evil, we find that it exists from the very beginning according to the creation stories."[9] But this is precisely what the Bible does *not* say; Yahweh repeatedly declares that all is "good" and even "very good." Exum's reading is not of Genesis, but of Genesis transformed in the direction of Hesiod's *Theogony*. Her arguments to establish the parameters of tragedy thus have the effect of subverting her claim that the Bible endorses a tragic outlook. Her claim that portions of the Bible manifest a tragic sensibility is sustainable only if one is willing to adjust the orthodox doctrine of creation, sin, and salvation.

The same criticism can be lodged against the work of Donald M. MacKinnon, who argues in a more philosophical vein that the gospel is itself a tragic narrative. According to MacKinnon, the gospel should not be read as a narrative with a happy ending, nor should the resurrection be seen as Jesus' belated response to the challenge to "come down from the cross." Every doctrine of atonement or resurrection fails if it "encourages the believer to avert his attention from

[8] Exum, *Tragedy*, 10.
[9] Ibid., 9.

the element of sheer waste, the reality of Christ's failure." Most especially, this failure is seen in Jesus' "abdication of responsibility for
his people's welfare" in the way He chose to address the doom that He
saw looming over Israel's future. By choosing the path He did, Jesus
"involved many of his contemporaries in a terrible guilt and provided
inevitably an excuse for his followers in later years to fasten responsibility for the crucifixion upon the Jewish people and their descen-
dants." This anti-Semitism, already evident in the New Testament,
comes to fullest expression in the final solution.[10] Victory though it
may be, Christ's work is also tragic, in the sense that the victory
comes at an appalling cost, in that MacKinnon comes close to blam-
ing Jesus for Nazism.[11]

In order to sustain this tragic telling of Jesus' life, however,
MacKinnon must delete or ignore portions of the gospels that he
finds overly "apologetic." Particularly in Luke and Acts, he writes,
Christian writers succumb to the "devastating intellectual and spiritual temptation . . . of presenting the catastrophic course of events
as expressive of the working of a traceable providential order."[12]
MacKinnon's hostility to the evangelists' "apologetic" efforts is
grounded in his supposition that the "doctrine" of the atonement is
"projected" from the raw data of history.[13] Obviously, however, the
facts of the gospel narrative do not come to us naked, but clothed in
the theologically charged language of the gospel writers themselves.
By assuming that he is working with "raw data" that can be given a
variety of different constructions, MacKinnon simply substitutes for
the gospel narratives a different narrative more in keeping with
MacKinnon's tragic sensibilities. To do that, however, is to change the
theological force of the gospel itself, for the gospel narrative itself is

---

[10] "Atonement and Tragedy," in MacKinnon, *Borderlands of Theology and Other Essays* (Phila-
delphia: J.B. Lippencott, 1968), 103.

[11] MacKinnon, *The Problem of Metaphysics* (Cambridge: Cambridge Univ. Press, 1974),
131–133.

[12] *The Problem of Metaphysics*, 129.

[13] "Atonement and Tragedy," 102–103.

not "data" for a doctrine of atonement but is itself a doctrine of atonement. MacKinnon's handling of the gospels supports John Milbank's suspicion that MacKinnon does not discover "history to be tragic" but "also *emplots* history within a privileged tragic framework."[14]

Both MacKinnon and Nicholas Lash use tragedy as a weapon with which to attack "totalizing" schemes that would smooth out the angularities of actual human history, but David Hart shows that the ancient tragic vision was itself a totalizing scheme, both intellectually and politically. If, as in Lash's reading of the gospel, the resurrection simply eternalizes the cross, then the cross is not the beginning of a new creation and not a critique of existing ideologies and social structures. Instead, for Lash, the God of Israel becomes the chief underwriter for the sacrificial economy of ancient tragedy, which can only mean that the sacrificial order is eternally validated.[15] MacKinnon's and Lash's tragic reading of the gospel, therefore, cannot be accepted without undoing the gospel itself. Contrary to their professed intentions, their tragic gospel actually gives aid and security to the totalizing schemes of antiquity.

Perhaps the most thoroughgoing Christian defenses of tragedy comes from Simone Weil, though, even more radically than with MacKinnon, that defense comes at considerable cost to her orthodoxy. As Katherine Brueck points out in her study of Weil's theory,[16] Weil recognized that what was at stake in a discussion of tragedy is not simply the question of God's justice but also the doctrine of creation. For Weil, the question was how to reconcile a world that is manifestly unjust in its distribution of rewards and punishments, and self-evidently indifferent to moral considerations, with a belief in a benevolent and powerful Creator. Can tragedy survive the Christian doctrine of a good creation by a good Creator?

---

[14] Milbank, "'Between Purgation and Illumination': A Critique of the Theology of Right," in Kenneth Surin, ed., *Christ, Ethics, and Tragedy: Essays in Honour of Donald MacKinnon* (Cambridge: Cambridge Univ. Press, 1989), 178.

[15] *Beauty of the Infinite,* 383, 386, 389.

[16] *The Redemption of Tragedy: The Literary Vision of Simone Weil* (Albany, N.Y.: SUNY, 1995), chap. 2. My account of Weil's tragic vision is essentially a summary of Brueck's chapter.

Weil believed that it could, but to reconcile Christianity and tragedy, she makes significant adjustments to orthodox Christianity. She
distinguished between exoteric and esoteric versions of Christianity. The exoteric direction of Christianity is "legalistic" and "egocen-
tric," and in this version the Christian seeks God hoping for the
reward of eternal life. In the mystical esoteric tradition, however, the
Christian seeks God without concern for reward and without hope
of establishing his merit before God. He seeks God for God's own
sake. In the exoteric tradition, it is important to believe that rewards
and punishments will be distributed equitably; in the esoteric tradition, there is no need for discernable justice in rewards and punishments. The exoteric tradition equates God's justice with a rationally
defensible distribution of rewards; the esoteric tradition says that
God's justice and goodness transcends all human standards of justice.
For the esoteric tradition, there is no hope for external victories,
which are partial and impermanent in any case; rather, we hope for
"interior victory in outer defeat," an interior victory that opens us
to love for the world through the experience of suffering.

Already it is apparent that Weil's theory is incompatible with the
doctrine of creation, being built on resentment against the limits of
creatureliness. Creatures, after all, are entirely and utterly dependent upon the Creator. To suggest that creatures might desire God
"indifferently" is to suggest that they can desire God without need.
But creatures are *nothing but* need, nothing but what we have received. Pious as it sounds to "desire God for God's sake," it is utterly
pagan and simply a pious gloss on the Satanic temptation to be as
God.

Creation is, according to Weil, organized to encourage people to
seek God without hope of reward. Weil reads creation through the
cross, and like the cross she understands creation as an act of kenosis,
self-emptying. When He creates the world, God "surrenders himself
to necessity, a force indifferent to the good and therefore foreign to
his own nature." More provocatively still, Weil suggests that the doctrine of creation *ex nihilo* means that God opens "a void" within Him-

self "in a voluntary act of self-emptying or withdrawal." God gives the world over to the rule of blind fate, and subjected to this force that has no concern with our moral character and recognizing that the world does not reward the good, we are forced to be good for reasons other than reward. His self-emptying withdrawal thus forces us to take the same kenotic pathway as we return to Him. What is required of us is a participation in the cross that involves "a horrific voiding of the personality in all its natural dimensions." God's goodness, in short, does not exclude but rather "necessitates a world where unmerited misfortune is a continual and serious possibility for every human being." Thus the cross, an event of suffering innocence, is the key to understanding Christianity in its essence and purity. The world manifests God's goodness and justice in that it "facilitates self-sacrificial love between man and God." If the world was set up differently, we would always be distant from God because we could never participate in the Son's kenotic love.

Weil thus sees total coincidence between the tragic vision and a cruciform theology of creation. As Brueck summarizes, Weil believes that two conditions must be met to establish the tragic vision and to support human love for God: "(1) The human race, by virtue of its very existence, is subject to blind forces indifferent to the good. These forces take the shape of suffering and evil. (2) Defeat by the exterior world provides the occasion for the human being's greatest victory. This is an inner victory which shines triumphantly in outer darkness."

How can Weil's "Christian" theory be reconciled with the prophetic eschatology summarized above? For the biblical writers, history is moving toward a deeply comic climax in which all wrongs are righted, all tears dried, and all losses regained with interest. Pain and the cross remain indelibly embedded in the narrative, and there is real waste and loss which is felt absolutely to be waste and loss. Yet, the final *telos* of the biblical story is absolute joy, peace, justice, and love. For the biblical writers, God's victory is without question a victory in the "exterior world," for the Fall took place in this world,

Israel was called in this world, Jesus was born, died, and rose again in this world, the Spirit came into this world, the gospel was preached to the nations in this world, and the new creation is a transfiguration of this world. Weil's esoteric and tragic eschatology is not a tolerable variation on Christian hope, but an explicit abandonment of Christian hope.

Weil's account is valuable not because it is good or true; in fact, in most respects it is bad and completely false. It is valuable, though, for displaying the inner connections between tragic vision and beliefs about creation, for highlighting the eschatological issues inherent in tragic wisdom, and for suggesting that heterodox beliefs about the Trinity underlie any conception of Christian tragedy (i.e., if the Father creates by opening a void and withdrawing, what happens in the eternal relation of the Father to the Son—is that also kenotic? On both sides?). Weil demonstrates that making a case for Christian tragedy (necessarily?) requires steps, large steps, in the direction of Gnosticism and trinitarian heresy. Weil's tragic Christianity thus leads us directly into the concerns of Part II.

II
Tragic Metaphysics and Theology

3
Metaphysics of Death

TRAGEDY IS A literary genre that normally describes the shape of epic, dramatic, or narrative plots. Insofar as our telling of history is "plotted," however, the term *tragedy* can be usefully extended to historical theories, and insofar as metaphysics and theology are ways of "telling the story of world," one can usefully describe certain philosophies as "tragic." Further, insofar as metaphysics and theology are ways of articulating one's deep sense of "how the world goes," one can speak of a "tragic sensibility" that is articulated in a "tragic philosophy." Though my use of the term "tragic" in this book is somewhat elastic, extending the meaning of this word is hardly novel. As Terry Eagleton has pointed out, tragedy "can refer at once to works of art, real-life events and world-views or structures of feeling." For many theorists of tragedy, "tragic art . . . presupposes a tragic vision—a bleak view of the world, an absolute faith for which you are prepared to die, or at least a dominant ideology to be heroically resisted."[1]

In the following pages, I explore some aspects of ancient tragic metaphysics particularly as they are manifested in tragic drama and philosophy. Tragic metaphysics runs parallel to and interacts with the tragic historical myths examined in Part I. I make no claims about causality. It is plausible that a tragic view of the movement of his-

---

[1] Eagleton, *Sweet Violence: The Idea of the Tragic* (London: Blackwell, 2003), 9.

tory provided "grounds" for a tragic metaphysics, but it is equally possible that foundation and superstructure could be reversed. My concern is merely to show that a common tragic vision animates the classical view of history and classical metaphysics. Much of modern thought, in its departure from Christian thought, is a reversion to these ancient tragic modes, and postmodernism has, if anything, intensified the tragic features of modern philosophy.

With the term "tragic metaphysics," I refer to two intertwined threads of Western thought. First, a metaphysics is tragic or a "metaphysics of death" when it interprets death as the final end of human existence, when it sees life as mere progress toward death, or when it treats death as a *necessary* boundary of life. Within the category of "tragic metaphysics," second, I also include philosophies that treat finitude, temporality, bodiliness, and limitation as philosophical and practical *problems* that must be either transcended or grudgingly accepted. Any metaphysics that treats "becoming" as a problem (which is to say, most metaphysical systems in history) is basically and inherently tragic. Such philosophies are tragic because they assess the world as if it were designed to frustrate human life and inhibit human flourishing. They are tragic because they believe the world has been designed to prevent man from realizing himself. Tragic metaphysics issues in a tragic ethics that kicks against the pricks of createdness, either resentfully or joyfully or resignedly. Gnosticism is one of the key illustrations of tragic metaphysics, for it sees creation as a tragedy if not a travesty. Ultimately, these systems are tragic because they refuse to recognize the world as a gift and to give thanks. They are tragic because they systematize the Satanic desire to be as God.

Finally, I assume throughout this chapter, as both a historical conclusion and a theological conviction, that philosophical and theological concerns cannot be separated. To say that Platonic metaphysics is a tragic metaphysics is to say that Platonic theology is a tragic theology. As this chapter progresses, I will offer occasional theological reflections on the issues raised by the tragic metaphysics of Greece, modernity, and postmodernity. As already suggested by the discussion of Simone Weil in the previous chapter, a tragic conception of history and life has much to do with one's understanding of creation, and that will be the focus of the theological comments in this chapter. Ultimately, the core theological issue is one of theology proper; creation is an aspect of trinitarian theology, in that the doctrine of creation requires a trinitarian theology. That central concern, at the heart of everything and lurking behind every corner of the argument in this chapter, will be my explicit focus in the following chapter.

I.

George Steiner has fixed on the connection between Greek religion and tragic drama to develop a wide-ranging assessment of the differences between the tragic outlook of Hellenism and impossibility of tragedy in the Hebrew worldview. Historically, he claims, the dominance of tragic literature in Greece resulted from the dominance of Homer, and especially the *Iliad*, which, from what we can tell from manuscript and literary evidence, was the most popular literary work of ancient Greece and functioned as something of a "Bible" for the Greek world. The *Iliad* forged the link between the heroism and the tragic ethos:

> It is impossible to tell precisely how the notion of formal tragedy first came to possess the imagination. But the *Iliad* is the primer of tragic art. In it are set forth the motifs and images around which the sense of the tragic has crystallized during nearly 3000 years of western poetry: the shortness of heroic life, the exposure of man to the murderousness and caprice of the inhuman, the fall of the City. [2]

In Steiner's view, tragedy assumes a certain view of the world, of God, and of divine justice. In the Bible, God is mysterious and unfathomable; He is not under our control. Yet, He is trustworthy and reliable, not because we can manipulate Him but because of the righteousness of His own character. "Tragic drama," Steiner claims, "arises

---

[2] *The Death of Tragedy* (New York: Oxford Univ. Press, 1961), 5.

out of precisely the contrary assertion: necessity is blind and man's encounter with it will rob him of his eyes, whether it be in Thebes or in Gaza. The assertion is Greek, and the tragic sense of life built upon it is the foremost contribution of the Greek genius to our legacy."[3] Steiner sharply distinguishes Greek and Hebraic conceptions of catastrophe:

> Note the crucial distinction: the fall of Jericho or Jerusalem is merely just, whereas the fall of Troy is the first great metaphor for tragedy. . . . The burning of Troy is final because it is brought about by the fierce sport of human hatred and the wanton, mysterious choice of destiny. . . . The Judaic vision sees in disaster a specific moral fault or failure of understanding. The Greek tragic poets assert that the forces which shape or destroy our lives lie outside the governance of reason or justice. Worse than that: there are around us daemonic energies which prey upon the soul and turn it to madness or which poison our will so that we inflict irreparable outrage upon ourselves and those we love. . . . To the Jew there is a marvelous continuity between knowledge and action; to the Greek an ironic abyss.[4]

One could say that for Steiner the difference between comic and tragic visions is a question of theology proper. The gods of Greek myth and tragedy are fickle and untrustworthy, and humans are little more than playthings in their hands. When a man confronts such gods, the Greeks believed, he is right to refuse to bow, and the tragic hero is one who remains unbowed before the "vengeful spite or injustice of the gods." Though he loses his eyes, Oedipus does not lose his air of command. Job stops his mouth, but the tragic hero refuses to submit. Tragic heroes—Greeks like Oedipus and Achilles and American tragic heroes like Captain Ahab—never bow before the gods of their worlds.

Following a similar line of argument but coming from the opposite literary pole, Michael Gelven has suggested that comedy depends on humility, the presence of grace, and the possibility of forgiveness.

---

3 Ibid.
4 Ibid.

[Both Christianity and Dionysiac religion] emphasize the immanence rather than the transcendence of divinity; they both center on an incarnate god, with a mortal mother and a divine father. They both seem to celebrate or worship with self-recognition of human folly. Grace, however, is much more prominent in Christian theology than in the Greek; and Shakespeare is simply a superior comedic genius to any Hellenic artist. . . . The Christian doctrines of the forgiveness of sins, the redemption, and above all the curious teaching that love is the nature of God's relationship to his creatures, creates a spiritual atmosphere that enables comedy in a very special way. Comedy may well be the preeminent Christian art form; and Christianity may be the preeminent spirituality necessary for comedy, especially comedic truth. . . . What enables us to reflect upon our weakness and our folly without dread? . . . It is the trust that comes from thinking on the supreme reality as a personal, and indeed loving, hence forgiving father. . . . [O]nly as fools graced by favor can we delight joyously in our truth being exposed.[5]

There is, I believe, considerable truth in these formulations, but, historically speaking, Steiner's claims are highly anachronistic. He defines tragedy in stark terms: "Tragedies end badly. The tragic personage is broken by forces which can neither be fully understood nor overcome by rational prudence." Steiner recognizes that some ancient tragedies end on a "note of grace," but asserts that these are exceptional. Disaster in tragedy is irreversible, even if at the end of the story things are not quite so bad as they could be. In tragedy, the situation cannot be solved by technical or legal means, and we never return to the *status quo ante*. Far less do we move forward to a new situation that restores all losses. There is no resurrection in tragedy: "Job gets back double the number of she-asses; so he should, for God has enacted upon him a parable of justice. Oedipus does not get back his eyes or his sceptre over Thebes."[6]

---

[5] Gelven, *Truth and the Comedic Art* (Albany, N.Y.: SUNY Press, 2000), 121.
[6] *Death of Tragedy*, 8.

Greeks, however, did not understand "tragedy" in these terms. In his study of Chaucer's notion of tragedy, Henry Ansgar Kelly writes,

> The selective introduction of Aristotelian criteria of excellence in tragedy has been a source of untold confusion in modern discussions of tragedy. For Aristotle, the "raw material" to be classified, that is, the mass of plays or stories already categorized as tragedies, was distinguished by "seriousness," and included a large number of cases with happy endings. In the Middle Ages, according to several authorities, the unhappy ending was one of the main generic distinctions of tragedy. This idea has become so ingrained in us that we tend to assume that it was also Aristotle's idea: that is, we assume that Aristotle was working from a medieval definition of tragedy, and we tend to edit out or ignore his recognition of tragedies with happy endings: especially, as already noted, his discussion in the fourteenth chapter of the *Poetics* where he says that a tragedy like Euripides's *Iphigeneia in Tauris* best achieves the desired tragic effects.

Our idea of what constitutes "tragedy" is thoroughly medieval, and Kelly argues that "It is Chaucer rather than Aristotle who sets forth the acceptable limits of our modern idea of tragedy, and it is Chaucer who can be said to have fixed these limits for the modern world." Chaucer's particular contribution was to recognize that tragedy involves something more than just punishment. Most medieval writers said that tragedies ended unhappily, but they meant that tragedies ended with "deserved retribution visited upon the wicked." Chaucer thought differently because of what he had read from Boethius:

> It was Chaucer's good fortune that he received from his Boethius glossator an unrestricted definition of tragedy, which left every sort of misfortune eligible for inclusion. Chaucer's definition corresponds to the modern everyday idea of tragedy, the range of which can be tested by considering the applications of the expression 'What a tragedy!'[7]

[7] Kelly, *Chaucerian Tragedy* (Woodbridge, Suffolk: D. S. Brewer, 1997), 139–140.

Steiner thus projects a Chaucerian view of tragedy on the Greeks, and then seeks to explain Greek tragedy by reference to Greek theology.

Yet, as I argued in chapter 1, the Greek vision of history was indeed "tragic" in a Chaucerian sense, and I argue below that Greek metaphysics was tragic in a similar sense. Life, the Greeks believed, inexorably and irreversibly tended toward death, and this trajectory toward the grave was understood as one of the deep structures of sensible reality, if not of the whole of reality. This somber view of the world was, further, reflected in the plays the Greeks called "tragedies." Yet, the connections between tragic metaphysics and tragic drama are not precisely the connections that Steiner and Gelven draw. To determine how the two are connected, we must briefly summarize the origins of tragic drama.

In a recent study of the origins of tragedy, the remarkable classicist Christiane Sourvinou-Inwood endorses the view of Horace and many ancient writers that our word "tragedy" derives from the Greek word *tragos*, meaning a male goat. The first hints of tragedy, she argues, are found in hymns sung to accompany the sacrifice of a goat at the Athenian festival of the City Dionysia. At the center of this festival was a ritual welcome of Dionysus to the city center (symbolized by a procession of phallic symbols), but the welcome of Dionysus was preceded by resistance to the god. Dionysus was a dangerous and unsettling god, a god of wine and sexual excess. Especially for those who held power, the coming of Dionysus was a potent moment, and permitting him to enter the city risked disorder and the loss of self- and civic control. The resistance to Dionysus's presence in the city is dramatized in various myths of Dionysus, most elaborately in Euripides's *The Bacchae*.

Paradoxically, the festival ultimately embraced the disorderly Dionysus not to undermine order but to establish it. Order was established not by resisting the god but by welcoming him, for Dionysus was, as Sourvinou-Inwood puts it in a nice phrase, "the teacher of controlling the loss of control." Dionysus brought wine, and with it the danger of drunkenness. But drunkenness resulted only if the drinker resisted Dionysus. If one accepted and submitted to the god of wine, then men could drink and yet learn to stay upright (*orthos*). Likewise, anyone who resisted the sexual disorder of Dionysus would lose sexual control and fertility, but those who submitted to the god could "control the loss of control." Worshipers of Dionysus would alone remain sexually upright (*orthos*), that is, "erect." (As Sourvinou-Inwood points out, *orthos* was sometimes used to describe a phallus held upright during a Dionysian festival.) Tragic drama thus arises in a theatrical and political context rich with theological and philosophical concerns. As Sourvinou-Inwood puts it, tragedy was a mode of religious exploration, which examined philosophical-religious paradoxes of order and disorder, as well as the unknowable and uncontrollable character of the gods. Her account makes it clear that theological, mythical, dramatic, "metaphysical," and political issues are all in play at the origins of tragedy.[8]

II.

From this angle, then, the concerns raised by tragic drama are the basic problems of Greek metaphysics, partially identified by Sourvinou-Inwood: chaos and order, civic life and nature, change and mutability, time, and desire. These issues, further, provide a window through which we can discern the links between ancient tragic metaphysics and modern and postmodern philosophical movements. Eventually, this set of questions will help us to see more sharply the contrast between the tragic metaphysics of antiquity and modernity and the comic metaphysics implied by trinitarian theology. In the remainder of this chapter, I examine how these themes arise, complexly tangled, within tragic drama especially, but also in Greek philosophy and political thought.

---

[8] Christiane Sourvinou-Inwood, *Tragedy and Athenian Religion* (Lanham, Md.: Lexington Books, 2003).

Order and Disorder

In several recent works, David Bentley Hart has pointed to the tragic character of ancient philosophy. European antiquity, he argues, was characterized by an ethos of "glorious sadness." Within the city, opposing forces of order and chaos were kept under control by a sacrificial mythos and praxis, which together warded off the destructive powers of nature and yet also won the divine favor necessary to keep the city functional. The same opposition of order and chaos, and the same sacrificial control, are evident in ancient philosophy. For the pre-Socratics, reality was "a kind of strife between order and disorder, within which a sacrificial economy held all the forces in tension." Platonic dualism, too, was ultimately tragic: "The world, for all its beauty, is the realm of fallen vision, separated by a great *chorismos* from the realm of immutable reality." Later, the Aristotelians' efforts to combine act and potency are inseparable from an inevitable process of decay and death, and Stoicism further illustrates the tragic character of ancient philosophy by positing "a vision of the universe as a fated, eternally repeated divine and cosmic history, a world in which finite forms must constantly perish simply in order to make room for others, and which in its entirety is always consumed in a final *ecpyrosis* (which makes a sacrificial pyre, so to speak, of the entire universe)."

Neoplatonism, Hart suggests, "furnishes the most poignant example":

> [I]ts monism merely inverts earlier Platonism's dualism and only magnifies the melancholy. Not only is the mutable world separated from its divine principle—the One—by intervals of emanation that descend in ever greater alienation from their source, but because the highest truth is the secret identity between the human mind and the One, the labor of philosophy is one of escape: all multiplicity, change, particularity, every feature of the living world, is not only accidental to this formless identity, but a kind of falsehood, and to recover the truth that dwells within, one must detach oneself from what lies without, including the sundry incidentals of one's individual existence;

truth is oblivion of the flesh, a pure nothingness, to attain which one must sacrifice the world.[9]

This metaphysics and politics are reminiscent of the tragic views of history examined in chapter 1: for Hesiod, later was necessarily worse; for Platonists and Neoplatonists, everything that derives from the One or the forms is necessarily decadent. Platonism is Hesiod's view of history turned vertically into a chain of being; Hesiod is Plato made horizontal.

Hart challenges the notion of tragic wisdom, claiming that what looks like tragic insight in Attic tragedy is really "emotional exhaustion": the chorus "foresees or fails to, it warns, it dreads, it ululates, but the only 'wisdom' arrived at from the choral vantage point is a state of resignation before the invincible violence of being." Sacrifice was a system for maintaining the *status quo* or restoring a *status quo ante*, and thus was hostile to "every motion outward, beyond the sentineled frontier, and reinforces the stable foundation of the totality."[10] Tied up as it is with the sacrificial economy of antiquity, Hart argues, in Giarardian accents, tragic drama cannot see any hope beyond a return to the origin:

> Whereas the resurrection of Christ in a sense breaks the bonds of the social order that crucifies, so as to inaugurate a new history, a new city, whose story is told along the infinite axis of divine peace, the religious dynamism of Attic tragedy has the form of a closed circle; it reinforces the civic order it puts into question, by placing that order within a context of cosmic violence that demonstrates not only the limits but the necessity of the city's regime.

What survives in a weakened form in the *Poetics* as the "pity and fear" aroused by tragedy was originally much more disturbing: "Behind Athenian dramaturgy lay memories of the promiscuous cruelty

---

[9] David B. Hart, "Christ and Nothing," *First Things* (October 2003), 49–51.
[10] Hart, *Beauty of the Infinite*, 386.

and antinomianism of the god who came out of the Libyan wastes to shake the pillars of the city, and the hope that, if this devastating force could be contained within the Apollonian forms and propitiated through a ritual carnival mimicking its disorder, perhaps the polis could for another year maintain its precarious peace against a world that is essentially a realm of countervailing violences."[11] Disorder is a violence against order, but order can be established, in the ancient system, only by violent suppression of the violence of disorder. Though Hart is speaking mainly of the "violences" associated with the metaphysical principles of order and chaos, the point holds also in the more directly religious sphere: a polytheistic world, after all, is by definition "a realm of countervailing violences."

Reinhold Niebuhr, along similar lines, recognizes that for the Greek tragedians, evil and hence tragedy was bound up with all human creativity: "The tragic poet could not get beyond the conception that evil was inextricably involved in the most creative forces of human life. From the standpoint of his conception life was therefore purely tragic." Creativity is conceived as another form of chaos, and dangerous to order. Tragic drama's fear of creativity is consistent with the metaphysical concentration on being: in a system where "being" is the highest good and reality, and being is understood as fixedly perfect being, immobile being, *any* becoming is tragic, a "fall" from the bliss of being. Since human life is necessarily a matter of *becoming*, since human life is a ceaseless "creation" of new situations and new artifacts, human life is necessarily tragic.[12]

Martha Nussbaum confirms that Greek ethics and politics were infused with the problem of order and chaos that animated tragic drama. According to Nussbaum, the problem of moral luck was at the center of Greek philosophical ethics, and she claims that "tragic" and "Aristotelian" conceptions of moral luck and the "fragility of

---

[11] Ibid., 373–394.

[12] Niebuhr, *Beyond Tragedy: Essays on the Christian Interpretation of History* (New York: Scribner's, 1937), chap. 8.

goodness" are at one. She cites Pindar to illustrate the problem: a good man is like a tree, Pindar claims, but if so, then the good man is dependent for his flourishing on all sorts of resources and "blessings" beyond his control—rainfall, winds, sun, and so on. Greek philosophy was an effort to find some ground for the good life that was *not* dependent on these external and uncertain resources, some mechanism for limiting the scope of moral "luck," some ground for the good life rooted in reason alone. As Nussbaum explains,

> However much human beings resemble lower forms of life, we are unlike, we want to insist, in one crucial respect. We have reason. We are able to deliberate and choose, to make a plan in which ends are ranked, to decide actively what is to have value and how much. All this must count for something. If it is true that a lot about us is messy, needy, uncontrolled, rooted in the dirt and standing helplessly in the rain, it is also true that there is something about us that is pure and purely active, something that we could think of as "divine, immortal, intelligible, unitary, indissoluble, ever self-consistent and inevitable." It seems possible that this rational element in us can rule and guide the rest, thereby saving the whole person from living at the mercy of luck.

Her book examines "the aspiration to rational self-sufficiency in Greek ethical thought: the aspiration to make the goodness of a good human life safe from luck through the controlling power of reason."[13]

These hopes are chimerical, of course. Nussbaum examines, for example, the role of social and political order as means of controlling luck. Being born into a stable society is one of those strokes of good fortune on which the good life depends. Think of the difference in the potential for virtue between a child born among the wretched Ik in the mountains of Uganda and one born in a secure suburb of Utrecht. Greek ethics, in Aristotle particularly, recognized that "trust" was essential to the virtuous life, and that trust was di-

---

[13] Nussbaum, *The Fragility of Goodness: Luck and Ethics in Greek Tragedy and Philosophy* (Cambridge: Cambridge University Press, 1986), 2–3.

rected toward the city's power to order the chaos of existence. So long as laws and conventions (*nomos*) are predictable and people abide by them, one can trust that there is hope for virtue and the good life. But *nomos* can fail, and then what? Tragic drama is frequently about what happens when *nomos* fails, and pointedly raises the question: Absent *nomos*, what is left to trust for the good life?

One response is to trust blindly, and against all experience, in the security of *nomos*. In a discussion of Euripides' *Hecuba*, Nussbaum points out that Polyxena, Hecuba's daughter who is offered as a human sacrifice by the Greeks to appease the shade of Achilles, goes to her death with great dignity and confidence in the conventions of society, the *nomoi* whose rules and distinctions structured life, whose guidance pointed to the society's chief values, and whose government of human responses of praise and blame shaped expectations. Nussbaum points to a particular scene to make the point:

> As she fell in death, reports the incredulous herald, even at that ultimate moment she took thought to arrange her skirts so that her body would not be revealed in an immodest way. This displays, of course, astonishing presence of mind. But it is even more astonishing for its display of trust. Dying, she does not think to doubt that a group of Greek soldiers will respect, after her death, the chastity of her skirt. If she acts well, she will stand, and be received.[14]

Plato, by contrast, addressed the problem of moral luck through his theory of forms, where all the most valuable and important realities were protected from the ravages of change and the dangers of bad moral luck. When he excluded poets from his ideal society, Nussbaum suggests, Plato was not only keeping certain genres of literature at bay but was seeking protection against the tragic potential of life. For Plato, "the best and most valuable things in life are all invulnerable," and thus Plato gets a kind of revenge against risk and the potential for tragedy that is unavoidable in the world. Plato thus

---

[14] Ibid., 405–406.

enables us to "effectively get the better of our humanity and keep for oneself the joys of godlike activity." Aristotle disallows this kind of revenge with its retreat from mutability, change, luck, and the risks of fragility. There is no separate realm of forms that is protected against the risks of moral luck, but that is no diminution of human life, Nussbaum argues, but an enhancement: "There is a beauty in the willingness to love someone in the face of love's instability and world-liness that is absent from a completely trustworthy love. There is a certain valuable quality in social virtue that is lost when social virtue is removed from the domain of uncontrolled happenings. And in general each salient Aristotelian virtue seems inseparable from a risk of harm. There is no courage without the risk of death or of serious damage." In short, "There are certain risks—including, here, the risk of becoming unable to risk—that we cannot close off without a loss in human value, suspended as we are between beast and god, with a kind of beauty available to neither."[15] Virtue and the good life are, for Aristotle, possible only in a world where evil is possible and where moral luck is always uncertain.

This is all very well-put, and it displays as clearly as one can the inescapably tragic character of life in Greek and, I would argue, in all non-biblical thought. Within Greek parameters, the problem of moral luck can only be addressed by Polyxena's dignified blindness to the collapse of *nomos*, or by the Platonic rescue of all good and true things from the risk of tragic outcomes, or by the Aristotelian conscious resignation to or embrace of the tragic. Christian theology, by contrast, has far richer resources for addressing this problem. Pindar's image of the tree is particularly apt, since it resonates with various biblical passages that describe the righteous man as a tree (e.g., Psalm 1). The biblical image of the righteous man as a tree has similar consequences for a conception of the good life, at least initially. It assumes, as Pindar's image does, that the righteous man is dependent on things outside his control. Yet in the biblical image, the

<hr/>

[15] Ibid.

nourishment of virtue/righteousness and fruitfulness does not come from undependable *nomos* or social relationships and institutions (salvation is not "through *nomos*," Paul insists), nor is security found in a protected realm of the forms. Rather, the Creator Yahweh plants the tree by the riverside, deeply rooted so that it will not be moved. Nothing is outside His control. For Scripture, even "bad moral luck" is under the control of a just God.

For biblical thought more generally, the problem of order and chaos simply does not appear. Creation is not a "taming" of chaos, not an act of violence against the violence of disorder. Creation occurs through speech, by the peaceful and utterly powerful *fiat* of an infinitely creative God. Creation is pure donation, not combat. All reality is gift, offered by a loving and faithful Creator, without the slightest shadow of chaos. All reality is ordered by His eternal decree. The world's pattern is so intricately constructed that we can grasp only a few pieces, but for Christians this realization brings no terror because we are confident all the other pieces will find their proper places.

Mutability

Nussbaum's analysis of the links between ethics and tragedy raises another crucial issue that is a slight but important variation on the theme of order and chaos: mutability, which was arguably *the* philosophical problem of ancient Greece. In his recent book *Death, Desire and Loss in Western Culture*,[16] Jonathan Dollimore argues that Western philosophy and culture have been defined by a particular linking of *thanatos* and *eros*, associated with the problem of mutability. When Yeats lamented, "Man is in love and loves what vanishes, / what more is there to say?" he was expressing a sentiment pervasive in Western literature and philosophy, sometimes shared by opponents in philosophical debates. For Heraclitus, reality was constantly in flux, and this flux must simply be accepted and even embraced. He understood

---

[16] New York: Routledge, 2001.

it not as harmonious change or dance, but as war and strife: "One must understand that war is shared and conflict is justice; and that all things come to pass in accordance with conflict." Order is an illusion: "The fairest order is a heap of random sweepings."

His philosophical "opposite," Parmenides, was equally haunted by the reality of change and mutability, but chose to deal with it through denial: the "It is" is "uncreated and indestructible . . . complete, immovable and without end . . . all at once, a continuous one. . . . Thus is becoming extinguished and passing away not to be heard of."[17] Platonism can be seen as a way of splitting the difference between Heraclitean becoming and Parmenidean being and stasis: the realm of forms is a Paremenidean universe, while the sensible world is Heraclitean. Aristotle was equally obsessed with the problem of change, asking how a thing can remain constantly itself through changing forms and appearances. He posited that a substance (an actual thing composed of form and matter) is the permanent "something" that endures, while "accidents" are the changing empirical properties of a thing. Aristotle's metaphysics, organized around the distinction of substance and accidents, is a metaphysics organized around the "problem" of change. Here we bump up against the tragic historical myths examined earlier, for the problem of change is nothing but the "problem" of time, which, for the Greeks, is inevitably the problem of death. Everything changes, everything moves toward death, everything decays. One can pretend that somewhere, somehow there is something that does not decay, and that perhaps somehow someday one will inhabit that realm. So long as one is in this world, however, there is no hope to arrest the slide toward death.

Ethically, the recognition of mutability in all things could lead in a hedonistic direction (eat, drink, be merry; *carpe diem*) or toward a kind of grim, Stoic resignation, but in either case the problematic is the same. The problem is in fact even more acute than that, for the realm of changeless stasis is itself a kind of death. Life means movement, and to the extent that movement is arrested in the realm of

---

[17] Ibid., 5–6.

the afterlife, it is not really an after*life*. The choice is stark: this world moves toward decay, the next world is motionlessly static. The choice is between life that moves toward death and death itself.

According to Dollimore, this concern with mutability comes to an even more intense expression in the Renaissance. Mutability is the background problem in many of Shakespeare's sonnets—time destroys beauty, the lover argues, and the lady is no exception. She will become old, dried out, and ugly. The only way to triumph over the ravage of time is to accept the lover's plea and have sex in order to produce beautiful children who will perpetuate the lady's beauty. The fear of "time's winged chariot" expressed in Marvell's "To His Coy Mistress" has a similar thrust: had we time to dally, we could wait for sex, but death is drawing near so we'd better get to it, and fast!

To the extent that mutability and change are problematic, to that extent Christian conceptions of reality have not been fully accepted or understood. After all, change is the story of creation from the first words of the creation account (darkness is broken by light, and then they alternate). At the end of the changes of each day of creation, Yahweh pronounces everything "good." Change can be, though it is not necessarily, good. Change *per se* is not a problem in the least, and for Christianity the ceaseless motion of the world is something to celebrate rather than mourn. Or, we can start at the other end: what we love dies, but for the Christian there is also resurrection, restoration, and complete final joy. That future hope throws the changeability of the world into a new light, and strengthens the Preacher's exhortation to "eat, drink, be merry, rejoice with the wife of your youth, and tell yourself your work is good" in the face of life's "vaporous" character. To the extent that Dollimore is correct, to that extent the Western world has remained a mishmash of Hellenic despair in the face of change on the one hand and Christian hope in resurrection on the other.[18]

---

[18] The great weakness of Dollimore's stimulating book is the complete absence of any consideration of the resurrection. He deals with Augustine as if he were an unreconstructed Neoplatonist, and gives medieval Christian thought virtually no attention at all.

Desire

The problem of mutability, as the Yeats quotation indicates, is also a problem of desire. If all life tends toward *thanatos*, this becomes acutely painful because of *eros*. Again, each horn of this dilemma gores. If we desire, we will end up bereft of what we desire. On the other hand, if we were capable of being consistent Stoics, our desires would conform to reality, and death and change would bring no pain. But that would mean giving up a fair bit of our humanity, for life is driven by desire and love. And besides—yet another horn, or back to the first one—few are capable of being Stoic. Desire for what vanishes is a torture, and that is simply the condition of life.

For some, desire *per se* appears to be inherently tragic. Desire arises from lack, because we only desire what we do not yet have. When our desires are satisfied, our lack is filled, and when all our desires are satisfied, then all lack is filled and we reach a static perfection. But this stasis is just another name for death, and that implies desire, insofar as it is desire for satisfaction, is always desire for death. Desire is the desire for the death of desire, and since all desires are ended by death, desire seeks death. As an alternative, one might say that desires (which arise from lack) are never finally satisfied. When one desire is satisfied, we immediately want something more, or want the same thing again and again. Because desire is never satisfied, we never reach satisfaction or fulfillment. Desire is always frustrated, and therefore our desires are always destined for tragic unfulfillment. Or, finally, desire—since it is lack—does both things simultaneously: as fulfilled, it leads to death; unfulfilled, it leads to frustration. Desire is doubly tragic, since it is always both fulfilled and unfulfilled. Desire is also tragic because of the problem of mutability: what we desire is no longer what we desired once we have gained it; because of the passage of time, it is other than what we first desired. A man sees a beautiful woman, but time changes her and before he can consummate his desire she is no longer precisely the woman he desired—not to mention the fact that he is no longer what he was when he first desired her. The wheel has turned; the river has flowed along.

This overlap of desire and death is part of the background for Dollimore's (quasi-Freudian) claims about the "eroticization" of death in Western culture. By this term, he refers to the tendency of Western writers (and visual artists) not only to describe death as a desirable erasure of desire (or desirable for some other reason) but also to describe death in quasi-erotic terms. This is seen in the "beautiful deaths" of ancient epic, most especially in Virgil, who shows an odd fascination with the pathetic deaths of beautiful young men, in the funeral customs of the Victorian age and after, in the pathetic death scenes of innocent (but always precociously beautiful) Dickensian children, in Poe's claim that there is nothing more poetic than the death of a beautiful young woman, in the fixed and eternal beauty of tragic heroines like Juliet, and on and on. Of course, there is also an important thread of realism in Western thought—death is just death, and it means corpses rotting and returning to dust (e.g., Achilles in the underworld in the *Odyssey*)—but the attempt to dress death in beautiful robes is a recurring theme of Western civilization.[19]

This "eroticization" of death expresses a paradoxical attitude toward death. On the one hand, death is too horrible to be looked in the face, but on the other hand death is prettied up so that it becomes attractive. This love-hate for death is one of the key animating dynamics behind classical literature, particularly heroic literature. Ancient heroes exist to gain glory on the battlefield, and the best way they can achieve that is to die a memorable death. They need and want death to gain lasting fame. At the same time, they seek immortality in the songs of bards because they know that the existence that awaits them after death is horrifying, and does not qualify as "life." They throw themselves into battle, seeking the fame that only death can bring in order to avoid the utter erasure of a death without glory—that is, pursuing friend Death in order to cheat enemy Death.

Along similar lines, Niebuhr has explained how tragic desire functions in ancient drama, highlighting its connection with the dialectic

[19] Dollimore, *Death, Desire and Loss,* passim.

of order and chaos. Tragedy arises out of the "hero's conscious affirmation of unconscious human impulses in defiance of society's conventions." He alludes to Freud, and perhaps the conception is more
Freudian than Greek (or perhaps Freud really did learn it from
Sophocles). In any case, the hero finds himself in a double-bind: the
hero acts on his impulses in defiance of convention and tragic consequences ensue; yet (and here is the really Freudian bit) if he fails
to act, it is equally tragic, for his desire is frustrated. The most stable
solution is the Stoic (and still somewhat Freudian) one: conform
desire to reality, or, failing that, accept the tragic frustration of desire with clenched teeth. Niebuhr summarizes:

> The tragic motif in Greek drama is . . . either Promethean or
> Dionysian (Freudian). In the one case the human imagination breaks
> the forms of prudent morality because it strives toward the infinite;
> in the other because it expresses passions and impulses which lie
> below the level of consciousness in ordinary men and which result
> in consequences outside the bounds of decent morality. The Greek
> drama thus surveys the heights and depths of the human spirit and
> uncovers a total dimension which prudence can neither fully com-
> prehend nor restrain. [20]

Theological issues lurk behind ancient views of tragic desire. We
may begin with the observation that the Bible does not present a
tragic conception of desire: Yahweh declares that He will give us the
desires of our hearts and that with Him is fullness of joy (Psalm 16:11;
37:4). He promises to fulfill our desires, so we can be confident that
desire is not tragically unfulfilled. Yet, in a biblical framework, fulfillment of desire is not tragic either, leading to a death-like stasis.
Within a Christian conception, the aporia, the apparent paradox, of
desire is not that it leads both to tragic fulfillment and tragic unfulfillment. Rather, since God is infinite and inexhaustible, the aporia
of desire is that we can be both fully satisfied in Him and yet look

---

[20] Niebuhr, *Beyond Tragedy*, chap. 8.

ahead to an infinite degree of greater satisfaction still to attain. We can hope for both satisfaction and the infinitely extended possibility of enhanced satisfaction, but this is without any hint of "dissatisfaction." In a Christian framework, desire is doubly comic: all wants are met, yet there is ever again infinite satisfaction still to be had.

Contrary to the common assumption, desire does not always arise from lack; in fact, desire may possibly arise from fullness rather than from lack. God desires the returning love of His creatures not because there is anything lacking in Him but because He desires to share the fullness of His triune life. So also, men and women may desire out of a fullness of being and life rather than lack. Because the claim that desire is inherently tragic depends on the definition of desire as lack, the argument falls when that definition is undermined. Further, in the Christian framework, perfection is not a static condition either for God (since He is [n]ever at rest) or for man (since, as Dante suggested, the more Godlike we become, the more we image the One who is pure act). Perfection or the fulfillment of all desire is not stasis, but boundless dynamic self-gift. Christian desire is then triply comic, since there are desirable goods that come only by giving—certain possessions, as Augustine said, that are only possessed by dispossession. Fulfillment of desire is in these cases comically enhanced by the opportunity to extend and enhance fulfillment of desire in others.

Christianity likewise challenges the eroticization of death. Death is not desirable, and desire is not desire for or toward death. It is one of the great contributions of late modernity (post-World War I) to destroy this lie. To the extent that postmodernism is a theoretization of death in *this* sense, it makes a resounding contribution to Christian apologetics, for it shows death to be utterly deathful, and shows that life outside of Christ is nothing but death.

Politics

In his rich study of Sophocles, Charles Segal has examined Sophocles' belief that political and sociological factors create the conditions for tragedy and furthermore render reality inherently tragic. Optimism gripped Athens in the Periclean period, an optimism about the ability of human *logos* (reason) and *nomos* (society) to stave off the savage potential of man's *physis* (nature), but the Peloponnesian wars, marked by several horrific acts of savagery (detailed by Thucydides), had an affect on Athenian consciousness not unlike the effect of World War I on the confidence of European civilization. In the aftermath of the wars, Athenian confidence in *nomos* eroded rapidly. Intriguingly, Segal points out that the meanings of *nomos* and *physis* exchanged places during the course of the fifth century B.C. At the beginning of the century, *nomos* was seen as liberating, a structure that suppressed the savage nature of man and enabled him to live in political community. By the end of the century, in an almost Freudian move, *nomos* is "seen as repressive and destructive" while *physis* had become a liberating principle. This is the ground on which the Sophists operated, bringing a "natural" critique against the injustices of the "legal" order. Part of the Sophist innovation was to argue that Athenian *nomoi* were products of human action and construction, rather than gifts of the gods, and therefore as susceptible to change and deterioration as any human creations. (Behind this, of course, is the Hesiodic and Ovidian idea that culture is a distorting supplement to pure nature.)

This was also the ground on which tragedy staked its claim: "The triumph over the beastlike life of savagery, so proudly celebrated by Sophocles in the *Antigone*, by Euripides in the *Suppliants*, by Critias in the *Perithous*, rings hollow when set against the recrudescence of bestiality and savagery in man's own nature. To this paradox the tragic poets return again and again." Euripides, writing in the midst of the shocking events of the war, depicts this dissolution of civilized order into barbaric bestiality; Sophocles, at some chronological remove from the war, deals with the issues more subtly, but still explores the limits on man's power to civilize himself.

A key symbol of this political and philosophical problem is the tragic hero's relationship to place, which, Segal points out, is ambiguous, symbolizing the hero's ambiguous social "standing." Places that should be safe havens become threatening (e.g., Agamemnon's bath), while places that seem threatening to others are the hero's dwelling (e.g., Oedipus exposed on the mountain). In part, this is because of the ambiguity of the hero's relationship to the *polis*. On the one hand, the hero's energy and physical strength is necessary for the survival of the polis; on the other hand, the hero's energy is so boundless that he threatens to break the order of the polis. There is a conflict, in Reinhold Niebuhr's terms, between the hero's vitality and the law.[21]

This is again the old Greek problematic of order and chaos being worked out in the practical situations of political life. Fixity is good; being is best. But being is static and motionless; the moment it moves it is decaying and dying. There cannot be any creation, any vital action, without breaking up the bliss of being, which is politically realized in the city. The argument is familiar from theology: change is either for the better or for the worse; God cannot get any better and God cannot get any worse, for then He would cease to be God; therefore, God is changeless. Or, we could transpose the argument into an exploration of the question of movement: movement is either to a better place or to a worse place; God cannot be in a better place than He is, and it would be unbefitting for Him to take a worse place; therefore God is motionless. Put in that latter way, it is clear that it is flawed, and it is flawed because it assumes the primacy of fixity and "being" rather than the priority of harmonious action. It assumes an unsupplemented origin, and assumes that any supplement means degeneration (see chapter 4). It fails to see that, as Barth said, the life of the triune God is a story. Scratching the sociology and metaphysics behind tragedy brings us right up to theological questions, questions that are insoluble outside a trinitarian framework.

III.

The Renaissance obsession with mutability shows that the dynamics of Greek tragic metaphysics were still at work, or had been revived,

---

[21] Segal, *Tragedy and Civilization: An Interpretation of Sophocles* (Norman: University of Oklahoma, 1981), 2–12.

in the early modern period. As Dollimore has discerned, this obsession with death, this tragic sense of life, is one of the hidden but crucial continuities between modern and postmodern sensibility. Modern tragic metaphysics introduces a new dimension to the problems of ancient and early modern thought; for moderns, time and historicity are threatening because they appear to rob human reason of its universality. If man is a temporal creature, his ideas are temporally limited and qualified.

Modern philosophy, most textbooks tell us, begins with Descartes's method of doubt and *cogito ergo sum*. Though Descartes's notion is seen as an epistemological move rather than a metaphysical one, it assumes a metaphysics. Seeking a secure and undeniable foundation for knowledge, Descartes subjected all experience and all life to systematic doubt. The one thing that survives the solvent of doubt is his own self-consciousness, for even if he doubts everything yet *he* is undeniably there doing the doubting. His self-conscious "I think" or "I doubt" becomes the foundation on which a philosophical system can be built. Though Descartes undoubtedly set a new course for Western thought, it was a shift within the overall system that we have been investigating. The *cogito* was a way of securing some space untouched by mutability, death, and tragedy. This motivation becomes clearer when we remember that Descartes was living during a period of horrifying upheaval and war that followed for a century after the Reformation. Recognizing that theological consensus no longer existed and therefore could no longer provide a foundation for social and political life, early modern philosophers and political theorists set out to discover secure foundations freed from theological commitments. Descartes's effort was the most successful of these.[22] In this context, then, Descartes's subjective turn is a version of the Platonic effort to secure some "place" of stability in the midst of a chaotic, death-filled world.

---

[22] For an analysis of Descartes that sets him in this political context, see Stephen Toulmin, *Cosmopolis: The Hidden Agenda of Modernity* (New York: Free Press, 1990).

Kant was more thoroughgoing in securing the subject against the challenges and risks of finitude. Kant's attitude toward temporality and finitude is profoundly ambiguous. On the one hand, in rebutting both dogmatists and skeptics, Kant argued that finitude was the condition for the possibility of universal and necessary knowledge, yet at the same time finitude was threatening. While Kant exposed the finitude of human reason, he drew back from it as from an abyss: "The fact that Kant recoiled from the abysmal dimension meant that he was actually conscious of this finitude. The recoiling is not only a concealing of the finitude but also an unveiling of the abyss." The "transcendental subject" was Kant's device for avoiding falling headlong into the abyss of finitude and its associated relativism:

> According to Heidegger, the reason Kant recoiled from this step lay in his subjectivism, which meant that in the final analysis he could only think of time as a subjective form. According to Kant, the transcendental subject itself, as the timeless foundation of the whole of transcendental philosophy, stands *outside time*: "Pure reason, as a purely intelligible faculty, is not subject to the form of time, not consequently to the conditions of the succession in time. . . . The transcendental powers of the subject are "eternal and unalterable laws." . . . "Reason is present in all actions of men at all times and under all circumstances, and is always the same, but it is not itself in time."[23]

The alternative, as Kant saw it, was to accept that the reason of the transcendental subject itself is subject to historical development and change. However Copernican Kant's revolution may have been, it was (like that of Descartes) still a shift within a basic framework, a new development within a basically tragic metaphysics. It was an effort to rescue *something* from the chaotic, tragic world of becoming.

Following Kant, philosophers embraced what Kant had recoiled from, namely, the relativity and finitude of human reason itself:

[23] Jos de Mul, *The Tragedy of Finitude: Dilthey's Hermeneutics of Life* (New Haven: Yale, 2004), 94–95.

Kant's static notion of transcendental subjectivity was not unique; it was shared by many other thinkers of the Enlightenment. Enlightenment thinking was founded on a static natural order, indisputably expressed by the laws of nature. Human beings and society were also seen as predominantly ahistoric, the products of a uniform and universal human nature. This applied no less to the empiricists than to the rationalists. . . . In post-Kantian philosophy, however, the notion that human reason has a universal and timeless character was taken less and less for granted. The great interest in non-Western cultures in the nineteenth century that was expressed in the new science of cultural anthropology led to important modifications to the presupposition of the universal identity of human reason. Owing to the historicization of the worldview, the presupposition that forms of reason are timeless was radically questioned.[24]

Hegel is a key example of this trend. If modernity means the construction of all-encompassing, totalizing, self-legitimating theories, then Hegel stands as *the* modern philosopher, the modern of moderns against whom all postmoderns frame their anti-theoretical apparatuses. Hegel's metaphysics is a tragic metaphysics in both of the senses described at the outset of this chapter. It is true that Hegel viewed Greek comedy as the greatest achievement of Greek religion. Epic gods are already humanized, but the attribution of events to both gods and men makes epic religion an awkward affair. Tragedy, by contrast, brings the "depopulation of heaven," since the gods have a much less prominent role in the action. But the results of tragedy's supplanting of epic theology are not evident until the rise of comedy, which treats the gods as mere clouds and shows that man is the reality always signified by divine characters. Thus "the Homeric poems, the tragedies of Aeschylus and Sophocles, and the comedy of Aristophanes constitute together a dialectical movement whose general sense is the following: the return of the divine into the human."[25]

[24] Ibid., 97–98.
[25] Merold Westphal, *History and Truth in Hegel's Phenomenology*, third ed. (Bloomington, Ind.: Indiana Univ. Press, 1998), 189.

At a more fundamental level, however, Hegel is noteworthy for the explicit way in which he gives death a constitutive role in his understanding of life. Instead of maintaining Kant's dualistic solution to the problems of tragic finitude, Hegel incorporated the tragic into his account of the Absolute. In the Absolute, all contraries are reconciled, but short of the Absolute "we live stretched across a fierce dialectic in which identity is dependent upon otherness or difference—dependent, that is, upon what it is not." For Hegel, the negative of my identity is not something alongside and outside my identity, but is internal to it. At an ontological level, Hegel argues that "*being* presupposes *not being*, and vice versa." The negation of any being is not opposed to or exterior to that being, but becomes interior to it. Thus, "infinitude takes finitude into itself, and self-consciousness must risk itself in otherness, difference, and even non-being, in order to be and to know itself. Submitting God and eternity to the same dialectic philosophy, Hegel infiltrates them too with death."[26]

Hegel's is also a tragic metaphysics because of his ambiguous treatment of finitude, contingency, and temporality. For Hegel, finitude is "eternally self-sublating"—*sublation* being Hegel's term for the incorporation/destruction of a thing's negation into the thing itself. Thus, the nature of finitude is "contradiction—i.e., not to be, but rather to destroy itself—it is self-sublation . . . finite things have the form of perishing—their being is the sort that directly sublates itself." Or again, "The finite is defined as the negative. . . . The universal manifestation [of it] is death—the finite perishes." At the same time, because death marks the limit of finitude, it is also the gateway beyond finitude: "The sentient vitality of the single being has its terminus in death. . . . The whole realm of the senses posits itself as what it really is, in its demise. This is where finitude ceases and is escaped from." Or, more directly, "Death is both the extreme limit of finitude and . . . the dissolution of limitation. [Death is] the moment of spirit."[27] Connecting this with the release from finitude that we

---

[26] Dollimore, *Death, Desire, and Loss,* 154.
[27] Qtd. in ibid., 154–155.

experience in thought, Hegel adds that "The escape from . . . finitude in consciousness, however, is not just what is called death; the escape from this finitude is *thought* generally." The life of Spirit is found in death: "The life of Spirit is not the life that shrinks from death and keeps itself untouched by devastation, but rather the life that endures it and maintains itself in it. It wins its truth only when, in utter dismemberment, it finds itself."[28] Finitude means death, but the death that is finitude is of the essence of life.

Un-Kantian as he is, Hegel shows some of the same ambivalence toward temporality that we found in Kant:

> On the one hand, with historicity Hegel placed the abysmal dimension of time at the heart of his system; on the other, his system is the expression of a heroic attempt to suppress this dimension. Hegel himself uses the metaphor of suppression when, turning to Greek mythology, he compares historic time with the Titan Chronos: "In this way, the Greeks speak of the rule of Chronos, or Time, who devours his own children; this was the Golden age, which produced no ethical works. Only Zeus, the political god from whose head Pallas Athena sprang and to whose circle Apollo and the Muses belong, was able to check the power of time; he did so by creating a conscious ethical institution, i.e. by producing the state."

Suppressing time enables Hegel to protect his philosophy against the solvent of becoming: "Hegel's philosophy of history, despite the fundamental place he ascribed to historicity, does not lapse into relativism."[29] But the threat of relativism only looms because temporality and history are told as a tragic story.

Wilhelm Dilthey (1833–1911) can serve as a final example of the tragic metaphysics of post-Kantian modern thought. Dilthey, one of the fathers of modern hermeneutics, historicizes consciousness and reason in a radical way, arguing that worldviews are unavoidable, yet

[28] Qtd. in ibid., 155.
[29] De Mul, *Tragedy of Finitude*, 106–107.

historically conditioned, and therefore relative. Of course, if that is the case, then Dilthey's meta-worldview by which he examines "worldviews" is also historically conditioned and relative, a point that Dilthey concedes. Recognizing this relativity, however, is the beginning of a great exodus for the benighted human race: "Historical consciousness breaks the last chains that philosophy and natural science could not tear. Man is liberated at last."[30] Yet, Dilthey also believes that this liberation comes at a cost: "Dilthey repeatedly observes that it is humanly impossible to continually live in the consciousness of the relativity of our most fundamental presuppositions. Should we continually admit this realization, every action and every thought would be paralyzed." It is thus essential for man to "think and act *as if* he is creating eternal truths and values."[31] As we are liberated by consciousness of the historical character of our consciousness, it comes into conflict with creative power:

> Herein lies the eternal contradiction between the creative and the historical consciousness. The former naturally tries to forget the past and to ignore the better in the future. But the latter lives in the synthesis of all times, and it perceives in all individual creation the accompanying relativity and transience. This contradiction is the silently borne affliction most characteristic of philosophy today. For in the contemporary philosopher his own creative activity is co-present with the historical consciousness, since at present his philosophy without this would embrace only a fragment of reality. He must recognize his creative activity as a part of the historical continuum, in which his consciousness produces something dependent.[32]

This is another variation on the ancient tragic dilemma of creativity and convention that Niebuhr identified. And it is an "affliction" only if time itself is an affliction.

---

[30] Qtd. in ibid., 280–281.
[31] Ibid., 281–282.
[32] Qtd. in ibid., 282.

Despise his insistence on the temporality and historicity of consciousness, therefore, Dilthey still considers temporality to be tragic, and he escapes this tragedy only by waving his hands and pretending that certain human acts, somehow, can transcend the temporal flow: "Man, as a creature of time, derives, as long as he acts in time, the certainty of his existence from the fact that he lifts his creations above the stream of time: in this light he creates more cheerfully and powerfully. Here we find the eternal contradiction between the creative mind and the historical consciousness."[33] Modernity, for Dilthey, did not invent this contradiction; it is a basic structure of reality. Yet, modernity is particularly tragic because it recognizes the distance between finitude and historicity on the one hand and the ultimately unachievable hope for infinitude on the other:

> What distinguishes the modern period—the period in which this metaphysical hope is becoming conscious of its historicity—from the preceding period, and what makes it a tragic period, is that the eternal contradiction between human finitude and human longing for infinitude, which in the metaphysical tradition was concealed by the metaphysical hope of being able to satisfy this longing, is now out in the open. Only now is human finitude a *tragic* life experience.[34]

Insofar as it is a development beyond modernity, postmodernity simply intensifies and makes explicit these same tragic themes. After Christendom retreats, modernity and postmodernity offer, in Hart's words, the alternatives of tragic joy and tragic melancholy. Nietzsche, the granddaddy of postmodernism, opted for tragic joy, embracing a strong pessimism that celebrated the tragic. He discerned that change and time were central problems in earlier Western philosophy, and instead of seeking solace in some realm of the unchangeable, embraced mutability:

---

[33] Qtd. in ibid., 356.
[34] Ibid.

As he puts it in *The Will to Power*, philosophers fear "appearance, change, pain, death, the corporeal, the senses, fate and bondage, the aimless." And this, for Nietzsche, is the underlying problem; we remain "entangled in error, *necessitated* to error, to precisely the extent that our prejudice in favour of reason compels us to posit unity, identity, duration, substance, cause, materiality, being."[35]

In embracing and celebrating mutability, however, Nietzsche was consciously embracing death. This is a remarkable move; Nietzsche is no Stoic enduring the inevitability of death and change, nor even an Epicurean who celebrates in blissful forgetfulness of death. He encourages a self-aware embrace of the tragic unprecedented in Western thought. Fundamentally, though, Nietzsche is merely repeating, with greater intensity, the claims about reality dominant in European thought since the Greeks. Life moves toward death, death reigns. The only change, and it is a remarkable one, comes in the Dionysiac celebration of the tragic condition of life:

> For a brief moment we become, ourselves, the primal Being, and we experience its *insatiable* hunger for existence. Now we see the struggle, the pain, the destruction of appearances, as necessary, because of the constant proliferation of forms pushing into life, because of the extravagant fecundity of the world-will. We feel the furious prodding of this travail *in the very moment* in which we become one with the immense lust for life and are made aware of the eternity and indestructibility of that lust.[36]

The world is fecund, and that necessitates a Dionysian embrace of the pain of mutability. But still mutability is pain, and the world is tragically structured.

The choice as Nietzsche saw it was very much a choice between the spirit of tragedy, Dionysius, and the spirit of Christ:

---

[35] Dollimore, *Death, Desire and Loss*, 245.
[36] Qtd. in ibid., 237.

Dionysus versus the "Crucified": there you have the antithesis. It is *not* a difference in regard to their martyrdom—it is a difference in the meaning of it. Life itself, its eternal fruitfulness and recurrence, creates torment, destruction, the will to annihilation. In the other case, suffering—the "Crucified as the innocent one"—counts as an objection to this life, as a formula for its condemnation. —One will see that the problem is that of the meaning of suffering: whether a Christian meaning or a tragic meaning. In the former case, it is supposed to be the path of a holy existence; in the latter case, being is counted as *holy enough* to justify even a monstrous amount of suffering. The tragic man affirms even the harshest suffering: he is sufficiently strong, rich, and capable of deifying to do so. The Christian denies even the happiest lot on earth: he is sufficiently weak, poor, disinherited to suffer from life in whatever form he meets it. The god on the cross is a curse on life, a signpost to seek redemption from life; Dionysus cut to pieces is a *promise* of life: it will be eternally reborn and return again from destruction.[37]

The postmodern obsession with violence, which is seen as inherent in life and language, offers another example of the essentially tragic character of the postmodern vision. As David Hart has argued, Emmanuel Levinas's ethics are ethics for a world without hope, and Hart sees his philosophy structured by an exile without hope of re-entry, in contrast to the traditional conception of emanation and return. Levinas attempts to stand resolutely against any "totalizing scheme," insisting that the Other is always wholly Other, and never reducible to the violence of the Same. The Other is so wholly other that it can only break into experience as "absolute contrariety," and this means that "the good can enter being only over against being" and the realm of being is "sealed upon itself" in absolute dualistic opposition to the "Other." What exists in the realm of "totality," which Levinas renounces, is reciprocity, longing for shared happiness, desire for another's love—in short, many of the constituent elements

---

[37] Qtd. in Hart, *Beauty of the Infinite*, 97.

of community. Levinas renounces these things because of their totalizing potential; community, after all, can degenerate into vicious
tribalism. But this need not be so, one would think, except that
Levinas has set up his system so that worldly existence is irreconcil-
able to the highest good. As Hart says, for Levinas, "if one cannot—
must not—see the good, but elects to serve it, terror, paradox,
despondency, and tragedy compose the 'ethical's' inevitable atmosphere."[38]

At the other pole of postmodernism, Giles Deleuze follows a more
Nietzschean program of joyful embrace of the chaos. Yet, Hart discerns the inner unity of Levinas and Deleuze, of "pagan exuberance"
and "Gnostic detachment":

> Even the seemingly outrageous juxtaposition of Deleuze and
> Levinas—absolute antinomian affirmation of the world and infinite
> ethical flight from it—proves perfectly logical: pagans and Gnostics
> both assume the iron law of fate to operate here below and violence
> to be pandemic in the sensible order (the former simply choose to
> celebrate the terror and bounty of life, while the latter depart for
> the sheltering pavilions of a distant kingdom). Both these extremes
> must appear—tragic joy and tragic melancholy—and indeed fortify
> one another, once the rupture of beauty from the good has followed
> upon the withdrawal of being behind the veil of the sublime.

Other postmodern theorists also perpetuate the tragic metaphysics of antiquity and modernity. Regarding the structuralist Freudian
Jacques Lacan, Dollimore comments, "What I find in Lacan is an
overtheorized expression of something more significantly and rel-
evantly expressed elsewhere (in Freud and before)," citing Schopen-
hauer and Montaigne. He goes on:

> In this respect I believe he is symptomatic of a much wider tendency
> in (post-)modern theory. But in terms of his influence alone Lacan

---

[38] Ibid., 85–86.

remains significant for this study. By crossing Freud's death drive with the philosophy of lack and nothingness derived from Kojeve's version of Hegel (itself influenced by Heidegger), he continues to drive death ever further into being; now, perhaps more inexorably than ever before, death is the lack which drives desire. In doing that he also exemplifies another significant tendency in modern thought which I have already remarked, namely the anti-humanist wish to decentre 'man' in the name of a philosophy which is truly adequate to the complexity of being, yet which seeks to retain a residual human mastery in the very effort of articulating this complexity. . . . modern theory, having lost faith in older philosophical notions of truth, now half-settles for the mastery of a new kind of complexity which it partly produces in order to enable this performance of mastery. Phoenix-like, the omniscient, masterful and above all complex analytic of the modern theorist rises above his sacrifice of "man" to death.[39]

Dollimore discerns here the continuing Cartesianism of postmodern theory, that is, the continuing dominance of the "masterful" man, floating in midair above the fray and flux of life, a hypothesis that attempts, like Plato's theory of the forms, to provide a way of escape from tragic reality.

Postmodernism thus understood is in strong continuity with modern and even ancient themes, especially with regard to the dominance of death and the evaluation of finitude and temporality as threatening and violent. What is new is the systematic way this is worked out; postmodernism is a theoretization of the dominion of death. Moreover, this is perfectly suitable as a *non*-Christian analysis of a post-resurrection world. As Hart points out, the dominion of death outside Christ is infinitely sharpened by the power of resurrection within. Postmodernism is tragic non-Christian thought come of age; it has arrived at what Cornelius Van Til called "epistemological self-consciousness." All this puts in question Lyotard's claim that postmodernism is defined by its refusal of metanarratives. Perhaps

[39] Dollimore, 196–97.

the particular metanarratives of Marx, Freud, and Hegel have been jettisoned (perhaps not, though), but it seems that they have been rejected in favor of another metanarrative. For some postmodern theorists, the story of Western philosophy culminates in *them*, and the narrative thus legitimizes the postmodern project. But that project is simply an intensification and "ontologizing" of the problematics of decay, death, mutability, order/disorder, and desire that have dominated Western thought from the beginning.

The conclusion of the matter is this: for the ancients, for moderns, and for postmoderns, human existence is fundamentally tragic. The world is built for tragedy. As a matter of sheer observation, we all die, and this is one of the few things that can be guaranteed about life. Time marches toward death, and in the end we all die. Change can perhaps be good, but change is ultimately decay, because in the end we all die. Desire is either fulfilled in a motionless stasis that might as well be death, or is never fulfilled, leaving us frustrated, and in the end we all die. Law gives a semblance of order to the process of decay and the forces of chaos, but law is uncertain, and in the end we all die. With their tragic narratives of human history, Hesiod and Ovid give mythical expression to the story of the world that ancient, modern, and postmodern all tell.

Apart from the gospel, what other story is there?

4

Supplement at the Origin

NO CONTEMPORARY writer has illumined the fundamentals of ancient and modern "tragic metaphysics" as simply and importantly
as Jacques Derrida, known best as the "founder" of deconstruction.
Derrida, however, uses the terminology of "supplementarity" in place
of the dramatic metaphor that I have been employing. I suggested in
the last chapter that Plato, recognizing that the sensible world moved
toward death, attempted to rescue some stability and fixity through
his theory of forms. Derrida tells this same story using different terminology. On Derrida's reading, "Platonism" (and by this he means
the entire Western metaphysical tradition) assumes that any departure from or addition to a pure origin is necessarily a regression, an
exile, a "fall."[1] Any supplement is necessarily a violent supplement,

---

[1] Derrida has discussed the problem of supplementarity in many works, particularly *Of
Grammatology,* trans. Gayatri Chakravorty Spivak (Baltimore: Johns Hopkins, 1976); *Writing and Difference,* trans. Alan Bass (London: Routledge, 1978), especially chap. 4; *Disseminations,* trans. Barbara Johnson (Chicago: University of Chicago Press, 1981), 63–171. I
will be concentrating primarily on the last of these sources. In this chapter, I am not con-
cerned with the accuracy of Derrida's reading of the Western tradition; I am more inter-
ested in Derrida, Derrida's Socrates, the way he exposes the tragic mentality underlying
"Platonism," and the open door he leaves for a trinitarian response. For theological cri-
tiques of Derrida, see John Milbank, *Theology and Social Theory: Beyond Secular Reason* (Oxford: Blackwell, 1990), 307–311; James K. A. Smith, *The Fall of Interpretation: Philosophical
Foundations for a Creational Hermeneutic* (Downers Grove: InterVarsity, 2000), 115–129;
Kevin J. Vanhoozer, *Is There A Meaning in This Text? The Bible, the Reader, and the Morality of*

attempting to overthrow and dismantle the origin. Derrida thus brings out into the open one of the basic assumptions behind the problematics of mutability and desire that we explored in the previous chapter. Ancient, modern, and postmodern metaphysics is a metaphysics of death because it is a metaphysics that denies or laments the inevitability of supplementation. Derrida helpfully exposes and deconstructs this model, but at the same time—not surprisingly, given his atheistic assumptions—maintains and even intensifies its most tragic features. Because Derrida expresses this problem in quasi-trinitarian terms, he provides some of the elements for a trinitarian critique of tragic metaphysics, while at the same time opening himself up in turn to a trinitarian critique.

In this chapter, I will first summarize Derrida's treatment of supplementarity, an exploration that will lead us directly into trinitarian theology, which deconstructs Derrida as residually Platonic. At that point, I change the key signature to show briefly how Derrida's description of supplementarity is lurking behind the tragic metaphysics examined in chapter 3.

I.

Derrida's fullest treatment of supplementarity takes place in connection with the Western tradition's treatment of the relation of speech and writing, which takes its cues from Socrates' account in the *Phaedrus*. Speech is the "original" form of language, while writing is considered to be a derivative and somewhat degenerate "supplement." To explain the problems of writing, Socrates appealed to the Egyptian myth of Theuth (or Thoth) concerning the origins of written letters:

At the Egyptian city of Naucratis, there was a famous old god, whose name was Theuth; the bird which is called the Ibis is sacred to him,

Literary Knowledge (Grand Rapids: Zondervan, 1998), 48–69; and Brian D. Ingraffia, *Postmodern Theory and Biblical Theology* (Cambridge: Cambridge University. Press, 1995), Part III.

and he was the inventor of many arts, such as arithmetic and calcu-
lation and geometry and astronomy and draughts and dice, but his
great discovery was the use of letters. Now in those days the god
Thamus was the king of the whole country of Egypt; and he dwelt
in that great city of Upper Egypt which the Hellenes call Egyptian
Thebes, and the god himself is called by them Ammon. To him came
Theuth and showed his inventions, desiring that the other Egyptians
might be allowed to have the benefit of them; he enumerated them,
and Thamus enquired about their several uses, and praised some of
them and censured others, as he approved or disapproved of them.
It would take a long time to repeat all that Thamus said to Theuth in
praise or blame of the various arts. But when they came to letters,
This, said Theuth, will make the Egyptians wiser and give them better memories; it is a specific both for the memory and for the wit.
Thamus replied: O most ingenious Theuth, the parent or inventor
of an art is not always the best judge of the utility or inutility of his
own inventions to the users of them. And in this instance, you who
are the father of letters, from a paternal love of your own children
have been led to attribute to them a quality which they cannot have;
for this discovery of yours will create forgetfulness in the learners'
souls, because they will not use their memories; they will trust to
the external written characters and not remember of themselves.
The specific which you have discovered is an aid not to memory, but
to reminiscence, and you give your disciples not truth, but only the
semblance of truth; they will be hearers of many things and will have
learned nothing; they will appear to be omniscient and will generally know nothing; they will be tiresome company, having the show
of wisdom without the reality.[2]

Writing is problematic for a number of reasons. Theuth's sales-
manship notwithstanding, King Thamus recognizes that the effect of
writing will not be to enhance or improve memory but to undermine it. Men who read books will not be wise, but pseudo-wise,
having the appearance of wisdom without its reality. Writing lacks
breath (*pneuma*, also "spirit") and thus is necessarily dead discourse.

---

[2] Translated by B. Jowett, <http://ccat.sas.upenn.edu/jod/texts/phaedrus.html>.

Writing, further, detaches knowledge from immediate presence of the teacher or writer, which raises problems both practical and theoretical. Practically, a written work wanders off to be read by any and everyone, regardless of their ability to read well: who knows what horrors of criticism a bad reader will concoct? Theoretically, for the Western tradition, the detachment of writing from presence means that writing is two removes from reality. Derrida's Plato imagines a world where thought is uncontaminated by writing, or supplemental commentary of any kind, a world where thought is pure thought, where the speech, emanating from the present speaker, stands transparent and obvious for all, no additions, questions, or interpretation necessary. This is the world of the forms, where things are real. The sensible realm, which contains only copies of real things, is the realm of supplementation, interpretation, and writing. Derrida cites Aristotle's famous formulation of the relationship between ideas and signs, to the effect that spoken words are symbols of ideas while written words are symbols of the aural symbols of speech. Derrida also points out that Socrates makes explicit connections between writing and painting, and what Plato's Socrates says elsewhere about tragedy, poetry, and visual art is applicable to writing: all of them, because they are two removes from the real, are distorting. Writing is necessarily a lie. So, for Derrida's Plato, writing (and with it all forms of supplementation) are forms of violence against the origin.

Derrida rejects the Platonic privileging of speech to writing not in order to reverse the hierarchy but in order to demonstrate that the problematics of supplementarity apply as much to speech as to writing, that supplementarity is the hidden story of reality. A physical example will help make the point. A spring, we say, is the "origin" of a small stream. But that "origin" does not exist as an origin unless there is a stream coming from it. If the spring is dry, there is no stream, and therefore no origin to the stream. As soon as the spring starts flowing, there is a "supplemental" flow—the stream itself. In short, there is no "origin" at all unless the "supplement" is there too. Supplements are not "added" to a preexisting origin, since the origin and the supplement come into existence at precisely the same time, and are mutually defining. Derrida himself cites Rousseau's insight into the problems of "nature" as a test and origin of human life. Rousseau wanted to celebrate nature, but recognized that nature is not a complete system in itself, but has an "originary lack" that must be fulfilled by a "supplement." A mother's "natural" supply of milk may not be sufficient to feed her baby, for instance, and it may come about that she has to use "supplements" to bottle-feed the baby. Thus the supplement, which seems an unnecessary addition to a complete origin, is in fact necessary to the completion of the original thing. Plato's dream of pure thought without supplement, pure idea without speech or writing is no more than a dream. Contamination has always already begun. If we say "I just want to discuss the spring and not the stream," we are talking nonsense, because the feature of "stream-flowing-from" is part of the definition of "spring."

Derrida recognizes this in a more forthright way than Plato did, though occasionally Plato employed imagery that suggests some vague sense of the problem. Supplementation is always already at the origin; there is no pure "speech" or pure "presence" or pure "being." For any of these realities to exist and enter our experience at all, there must be something added. Yet, for Derrida, supplementation of the origin is necessarily a violent supplementation, an effacement and substitution for the origin. He does not deny that writing entails an act of violence; he simply says that all language, indeed all reality, has the character of "writing," so that violence is enmeshed in every aspect of life. Both in language and throughout reality, the supplement is equiprimordial with the origin, so that the origin is disturbed and disrupted from the outset. He "radicalizes" Plato by positing an inevitable, and inevitably violent "surplus at the origin."

At times, he expresses this inherent violence mythically. Expanding on the Socratic telling of the myth of Theuth, Derrida points out that this god was frequently involved in plots against his father and his brothers:

This process of substitution, which thus functions as a pure play of traces or supplements or, again, operates within the order of the pure signifier which no reality, no absolutely external reference, no transcendental signified, can come to limit, bound, or control; this substitution, which could be judged "mad" since it can go on infinitely in the element of the linguistic permutation of substitutes, of substitutes of substitutes; this unleashed chain is nevertheless not lacking in violence. One would not have understood anything of this "linguistic" "immanence" if one saw it as the peaceful milieu of a merely fictional war, an inoffensive word-play, in contrast to some raging *polemos* in reality. It is not in any reality foreign to the "play of words" that Thoth also frequently participates in plots, perfidious intrigues, conspiracies to usurp the throne. He helps the sons do away with the father, the brothers do away with the brother that has become king.[3]

The god of writing (and hence of supplementation) is necessarily a parricide. It is as if the stream cancels out the spring from which it flows.

Like Derrida's deconstruction, Harold Bloom's theory of the anxiety of influence "theorizes" filial revolt. According to Bloom, all writers write against their predecessors, Oedipally struggling to escape their influence and master their "fathers." Virgil was haunted by the influence of Homer, simultaneously recognizing and resenting his debt to the Greek poet; how could Virgil achieve equality or superiority to Homer when he is so fundamentally indebted to him? How can the supplement (Virgil) secure his own achievement when he is always already only a supplement? Similarly, Dante works in the shadow of Virgil and Homer, and Milton in the shadow of the others. Each is attempting to overcome influence, so that true poetic creativity requires an act of patricide. Though there are clear parallels between postmodern paganism and the *Theogony,* Hesiod is a distant, very distant, influence on Bloom, Derrida, and postmodernism generally. A nearer influence is the radicalism of the 1960s. Derrida,

---

[3] *Disseminations*, 90.

Bloom, and a host of postmodern theorists treat "1968" as if it were not a contingent set of historical events, but as a moment of revelation, unveiling the constituent reality of things. For much of postmodernism, the story of reason is not, as Claudius had it, the "death of fathers" but the "revolt of sons."

For Socrates, written discourse is an orphan son, since the father does not remain present to "attend to it." Every son is necessarily a prodigal son, as Derrida expounds in a vivid and important passage:

> As a living thing, logos issues from a father. There is thus for Plato no such thing as a written thing. There is only a logos more or less alive, more or less distant from itself. Writing is not an independent order of signification; it is weakened speech, something not completely dead, a reprieved corpse, a deferred life, a semblance of breath. . . . It is not insignificant; it simply signifies little, and always the same thing. This signifier of little, this discourse that doesn't amount to much, is like all ghosts, errant. It rolls . . . this way and that like someone who has lost his way, who doesn't know where he is going, having strayed from the correct path, the right direction, the law of rectitude, the norm; but also like someone who has lost his rights, an outlaw, a pervert, a bad seed, a vagrant, an adventurer, a bum. Wandering in the streets, he doesn't even know who he is, what his identity—if he has one—might be, what his name is, what his father's name is. . . . Socrates' tone is sometimes categorical and condemnatory—and sometimes touched and condescending—pitying a defenseless thing, a son abandoned by his father. In any event the son is *lost*. His impotence is truly that of an orphan as much as that of a justly or unjustly persecuted patricide. In his commiseration, Socrates sometimes gets quite carried away: alongside the living discourses persecuted and deprived of the aid of a logographer . . . , there are also half-dead discourses—writing—persecuted for lack of the dead father's voice. Writing can thus be attacked, bombarded with unjust reproaches . . . that only the father could dissipate—thus assisting his son—if the son had not, precisely, killed him.[4]

[4] Ibid., 143–144.

The wandering son—the written text, the supplement, the "second" added to the "first," "becoming" added to "being"—needs his father for his own protection. Unfortunately, the father is not available, for the son has killed him.

II.

Throughout his treatment of supplement-as-son, Derrida is, probably consciously, playing with the traditional formulations of trinitarian theology. He apparently even comes to the Athanasian insight that the father necessarily has a son, in order to be father:

> The father is not the generator or procreator in any 'real' sense prior to or outside all relation to language. In what way, indeed, is the father/son relation distinguishable from a mere cause/effect or generator/engendered relation, if not by the instance of logos? Only a power of speech can have a father. The father is always father to a speaking/living being. In other words, it is precisely *logos* that enables us to perceive and investigate something like paternity.[5]

For Derrida's Socrates, the "father" is never approached directly ("no man has seen the father"), but only indirectly in the son. According to Plato, we have no direct face-to-face contact with the "Good," but only with the image of the Good which is the visible sun. But this son/sun exists to protect us from the face-to-face encounter with the Good, which would leave us blind. To the extent that Derrida examines the Western philosophical tradition in terms of father-son relations, he has, in some sense, carried on the Augustinian investigation of the *vestigia Trinitatis*, the marks and traces of the Trinity that are imprinted on reality. He shows that much of the Western philosophical tradition has puzzled over something like inter-trinitarian relations.

Derrida, however, is playing trinitarian themes against orthodox trinitarian theology. The *vestigia Trinitatis* he uncovers are distorted

⁵ Ibid., 80.

through a tragic mythology. This is most clearly evident in the fact that he describes the son as an inevitable parricide, always throwing off the shackles of the father in order to run free, always seeking the father's erasure. However much the father-son image may resonate with trinitarian terminology, it is clear that Derrida is far closer to Hesiod and Sophocles than to John or Paul. Hesiod described Zeus's aboriginal overthrow of Chronos in vivid terms. Chronos has been gobbling up his children, but Zeus defeated him first by trickery and then by superior strength:

> [Rhea, Zeus's mother] wrapped a large stone in babycloth and delivered it to the son of Heaven [Chronos], the great lord, king of the Former Gods. Seizing it in his hands, he put it away in his belly, the brute, not realizing that thereafter not a stone but his son remained, secure and invincible, who before long was to defeat him by physical strength and drive him from his high station, himself to be king among the immortals.[6]

This is the kind of father-son relation Derrida imagines between origin and supplement. But Derrida's preference of Hesiod over John raises a crucial question: If he is going to build his enterprise on mythology (which he would more or less admit), then why is Hesiod's mythology of parricide and filial revolt more compelling than the biblical story of filial obedience? Why is the tragic story preferable to the comic one?

For trinitarian theology the Son is not a veil over the Father's face but the very image of the Father who is perichoretically present in the Son. The Father is in the Son, just as the Son is in the Father, and this mutual indwelling or "perichoresis" is for John essential to the gospel. John begins his gospel by stating that "no man has seen God at any time" (John 1:18), and this represents a problem in John's scheme of things. For John, seeing is knowing (6:40; 11:45; 14:7),

---

[6] Hesiod, *Theogony;Works and Days*, trans. M. L. West (Oxford: Oxford World's Classics, 1988), 17.

and knowing/seeing the Father and Son *is* eternal life (Jn. 17:3). If the Son veils the Father, then there can be no way to life. Sinners need some way to behold Him. The good news is that there is such a way, and the name of that Way is Jesus. When John speaks of the invisibility of the God, he is not primarily making a philosophical claim. God is invisible (see Col. 1:15–16; 1 Tim. 1:17), but John's main point has to do with the progress of salvation in history. John first brings out a contrast of the Old and New in 1:14. The word translated as "dwell" can be translated as "tabernacled" or "pitched a tent." The eternal world has pitched a tent in human flesh and shown the glory of God. But when the glory came into the tabernacle in the Old Testament, everyone evacuated the tent (Exod. 40:34–38; 1 Kgs. 8:10–11). Now the glory descends in the flesh and "we beh[o]ld His glory" (1:14).

John is making the same contrast in 1:17–18, since the statement that "no one has seen the Father" refers back to the experience of Moses on Mount Sinai. When Moses asked to see God, the Lord responded that "You cannot see My face, for no man can see Me and live" (Exod. 33:20). Moses was therefore shown the "back" of God's passing glory, but not His face (Exod. 33:22–23). Having become flesh, the Word expounds the Father to us (1:18; see also 2 Cor. 3). It is thus no longer true that "no man has seen God." On the contrary, Jesus says that those who have seen Him have seen the Father (Jn. 12:45; 14:9) and claims that His words and works display the Father's words and works (Jn. 5:19; 12:49).

In chapter 14, Jesus goes further to explain that His "exegesis" of God is rooted in His eternal relation to the Father. The issue that dominates the discussion at the beginning of chapter 14 is the "way." Jesus has said He is returning to the Father (13:33; 14:2) and tells the disciples, "You know the way where I am going" (14:4). Jesus Himself is "the way" to the Father (14:6). And He is the way to the Father because the Father, the destination, is already and has always been "in" the way, that is, in the Son (14:7, 9–11). Jesus can show the Father because the Father is eternally, perichoretically in Him and

He is eternally in the Father. This point is reinforced when we consider what Jesus says about the "dwelling places" that He is preparing in His "Father's house." Though often taken as a reference to heavenly dwelling places, this is not what Jesus meant. Rather, the "Father's house" in John refers to the temple that is the body of Jesus (2:16–22). This is the "Father's house" in the sense that it is the place where the Father resides (14:10–11): the Son is the permanent and eternal "home" of the Father, as the Father is the eternal home of the Son. When the Son comes into the world, we get a glimpse of the "home life" of the Father and Son.

In the Incarnation, a window is opened into the eternal life of God. What is true in the Incarnation is true in the eternal relation of Father and Son. And what the Incarnation reveals to us is that the Son eternally lives to glorify the Father in the Spirit, and the Father to glorify the Son in the same Spirit. Jesus prayed, "Father, the hour has come; glorify Thy Son, that the Son may glorify Thee" (Jn. 17:1). Jesus has "glorified [the Father] on earth, having accomplished the work" that He had been sent to perform. The Father will now glorify the Son, but this is no new thing, since the Father glorifies the Son "with the glory which I had with Thee before the world was" (17:5). This glory is associated with the unity of Father and Son: "The glory which Thou hast given Me I have given to them, that they may be one, just as We are one; I in them, Thou in Me, that they may be perfected in unity" (17:22–23). We could hardly be further from Hesiod or Derrida. In the eternal life of God, there is nothing but mutual love, devotion, honor, glory, and self-giving. Jesus acknowledges that in the eternal life of God there has always been a "supplement," a Second and a Third alongside the First. But that Second does not murder, efface, veil, or undermine the First. In fact, the Second is never without the First, who is always with Him, even in His Incarnation, in perfect perichoretic unity. If this Son goes, as Barth said, into a far country, yet He does not become a prodigal, for the Father is always with the Son. In a trinitarian framework, there is no room for the tragic story Derrida wants to tell about origins and supplements.

Derrida's critique of Plato thus does not lay a glove on classical trinitarian theology. It is simply a heretical alternative to trinitarian theology. In its better moments, when it has been true to itself in dumping Plato, trinitarian theology has not dreamed of a world of pure origin or pure thought. On the contrary, confession of the Trinity is precisely confession of an eternal supplement, or rather, two eternally complicating "supplements," the Son and the Spirit. If there is indeed, as Derrida suggests, an analogy between Platonic metaphysical speculations and Platonic privileging of speech to writing, trinitarian theology simply rejects both. A trinitarian account of language can accept nearly everything Derrida says about originary "contamination," apart from the label "contamination." Here Derrida is truly Augustine's heir, for he has discovered a trace of trinitarian life at the heart of the Western philosophical tradition.

Why does Derrida continue to consider the supplement a contamination of the origin? If the supplement is "always already" there, why should it be a contamination of some pure being? Why should the supplement be a tragic and violent addition to the origin? The most convincing answer is that Derrida has yet to be liberated from the grip of the tragic "Platonism" that he criticizes so trenchantly. In trinitarian terms, the Son and Spirit are not contaminations of a pure, lone Father. The Son and Spirit are the fullness and glory of the being of the Father, without which the Father would not be Father. Without the resources of trinitarian theology, Derrida has nothing to call a supplement other than a "contamination." But a "supplement" contaminates only if Derrida is still using the pure Platonic origin as a standard of comparison. Derrida deconstructs Platonism as a mythology of fathers and sons, but in the light of a trinitarian analysis, Derrida turns out to be nothing but a Platonist with a bad conscience, a Platonist who wishes there could be a world of forms, talks about reality as if there were a world of forms, but knows that the forms are always already tarnished by their shadows.

James K. A. Smith comes to similar conclusions, though he traces Derrida's "interpretation of interpretation" to "the modern tradition

of immediacy." He sees Descartes's vision of a floating "ego" peek-
ing out from behind Derrida's deconstruction. Smith's analysis is
worth quoting at some length:

> Derrida is honest about not challenging for a moment Rousseau's
> and Levi-Strauss's reading of violence; his own analysis is only a
> "radicalization" of their thesis. . . . But as I have attempted to argue
> above, intersubjectivity is violent only if one maintains something
> of a latent Cartesian solipsism or egoism. But if, in contrast, we
> understand human be-ing as essentially inter-relational, then that
> may be understood as "good," as an instance of a good creation and
> not inherently violent. Admittedly, that is a "belief," but so too, we
> have discovered, is Derrida's interpretation.

Thus,

> [Derrida's] interpretation of interpretation as violent betrays another
> vestige of the modern tradition of immediacy, for it is only if one is
> looking for immediacy and full presence that the finitude of inter-
> preting "as" something is considered a lack, a fall, an impurity. The
> logic of supplementarity, despite all of Derrida's intentions, remains
> a kind of metaphysics of infinity. This is not to say that Derrida is
> looking for full presence or that he has any dream of immediacy, of
> escaping the interpolation of the postal system or of stepping out-
> side the space of interpretation. He has given up "any dream of a full
> and immediate presence closing history, the transparence and
> indivision of a parousia, the suppression of contradiction and differ-
> ence." The dream has died.

Nonetheless,

> its ghost continues to haunt [Derrida's] work. Of course, 'a ghost
> does not exist' . . . presence *is* not, is *not*, never was. But its ghost re-
> mains, a specter lurking behind his discourse, unwittingly shaping
> the plot of the story. A dream that has become a ghoulish nightmare,
> a recurring haunting of a nostalgic longing. . . . Derrida fails to see
> this phantom lurking in his own work, the "phantom of subjectivity."

Smith counsels that we simply give up the Platonic dream of purity, of unsupplemented and singular origin:

> But what if we were to give up an expectation of purity? What if we refused to be haunted by this ghost of full presence and gave up any pretensions to purity? Why must this be counted loss? . . . The decision is violent because it is finite; every decision is an incision only because it cannot measure up to infinity, "cannot furnish of itself with infinite information and the unlimited knowledge of conditions." . . . But is that not to make finitude a violence, and is this not violence only if we are expected to be gods, even if it is impossible—only a dead dream? What if, instead of construing interpretive decisions as finite *incisions*, the hemeneutical moment was understood as "all we have," an inescapable aspect of being of which nothing more is expected. . . . It is not a matter of "giving up the infinite" but rather of giving up the assumption that the only way to "do justice" to the infinite is to speak of it in its infinity—which, of course, is impossible.

From the perspective of the Christian doctrine of creation, finitude is good. Thus supplementarity, insofar as it is an inevitable structure of reality, is a "structure of respect." Smith asks, "Would not such a finitude be something like difference without being haunted by the ghost of full presence or the infinite ghost of metaphysics past?"[7] An affirmation of the goodness of creation and createdness, in short, would liberate Derrida finally from Plato's shadow. Derrida's work still partakes of the tragic metaphysics, the tragic conception of finitude, that we examined in the previous chapter. For all his postmodern posturing, Derrida is still too much the ancient, too much the modern.

Smith's point about the implications of creation are important. But the affirmation that creation is good is only possible as an affirmation of a trinitarian theology. For a good creation to exist, there must be a supplement at the origin. A (small-*u*) unitarian theology proper

---

[7] *Fall of Interpretation*, 127–129.

necessarily leads to a tragic view of creation, for anything that "goes out" from a unitarian origin is necessarily a diminished supplement, perhaps even a deicide. If a unitarian god could conceivably create (which is theologically doubtful), creation could not be a glorification of god. Unitarianism is inherently Gnostic, and Gnosticism is hyper-tragic, since it treats the creation itself as a fall, a tragic departure from an origin, an exile. For the Gnostic, to be created is to be abandoned, alienated, in a far country, and the only hope is return. Within a triune God, by contrast, there is always already a "departure," but a departure that does not involve any diminishment from the origin. The Son is equal to the Father in power and glory; the Father can beget a Son who does not diminish or veil His glory. This Son does not efface the Father; instead, the Father, though full of all glory, is ineffably, mysteriously "glorified" by the Son. Such a God can make a world that does not demand a diminishment of His being, since He has eternally produced a Son who does not diminish His being. The triune God, unlike Weil's tragic God, can create without kenosis, because He can beget without being diminished.

In fact, it is difficult to see how history can exist at all except as a reflection of the life of the Trinity. A story depends on initial breach, an initial move from the original situation. If there is no movement from the beginning, there is no story, but only stasis. The hero of the story must *do* something, and anything he does, anything at all, changes the initial situation. If history is to exist, there must be movement from the initial moment of history, some temporal supplement to the "Big Bang." For any unitarian system, that initial move is an exile, a degeneration, and the best that can be hoped for is a return to the origin. For any unitarian system—any metaphysics of "pure origin"—there can be no real "end" to the story. Further, there must be eschatology to get a story off the ground—somewhere to go, somewhere to arrive, which justifies separation from where the story begins. There is a teleology to every story—beginning, middle, and *end*—"end" here not merely meaning the last event but the goal toward which the story moves, the denoument, the climax. Especially a history that moves from garden to glorified garden, from Eden to New Jerusalem, requires a trinitarian God. A history that moves from glory to glory must be designed by a God whose glory flows out from the Father to the Son and to the Spirit. Given that history moves from this beginning to this end, God must be triune.

History is not a story of discrete and utterly unique events. History is full of pattern and recurrence, patterns of recurrence. The round of trinitarian life is also the background for the recurrent and cyclical nature of history, which gives history its particular texture. Just as the Trinity is the ground for metaphor, so also for typology. In the Trinity, we find the root of the "is/is not" character of metaphor. The Father is not the Son and yet if you have seen the Father you have seen the Son. And this positive-negative (which is not dialectical) is reflected in every feature of the creation. Creation contains objects that are really distinct and separate from one another. Day is not night, waters above are not waters below, water is not land, birds are not fish, and so on. At the same time, Scripture indicates that one thing can stand for, represent, or symbolize other things. Things in creation indwell other things. We say that a "righteous man is like a tree" not because we invent similarity between two essentially unlike things but because there is a real mutual relation between them. The Son is the express image of the Father, and yet is not the Father. This perichoretic "is/is not" (a man is/is not a tree) structure is inherent in God and is the very nature of metaphor.

And it is the shape of time and history as well. Time is divided into past, present and future, and yet these are not wholly distinct. Jerome Begbie has pointed out the analogy with music: the present moment, like a musical note, is what it is because of what has gone before and is in turn shaped by what comes after, so that every present contains within itself traces of the past and seeds of the future. This is not merely a subjective experience of "memory and desire" looking backward and forward, but is a feature of time itself (as it is a feature of music). The eternal background of this is again perichoresis: the past indwells the present, and the present will indwell the future. In fact, according to the New Testament, the present is indwelt also by the future, as the "age to come" becomes present in the power of the Spirit. The typological similarities between events thus depend on the perichoretic rhythms of the Trinity. The flood is like the exodus is like the crossing of the Jordan is like the return from exile is like Jesus' baptism is like Christian baptism. Such layering of historical events depends on a God who is always already One and Three. Thus, behind that affirmation of the goodness of finitude, of time, of becoming, and of original supplement is a trinitarian theology that affirms with Derrida that there is no simple origin.

To put it another way, the trinitarian life is a rhythm of self-giving and return within the life of God. Trinitarian life is life given over and returned as glorified life. The Father loves and submits to the Son, and the Son to the Father, and Son to the Spirit, and so on. But this self-giving of one Person to the others is always met with a return gift: the Father's gift of Himself to the Son is met with the Son's gift of Himself to the Father. "Self-sacrifice" is met with a returning self gift that eternally and ever refreshes and renews the triune fellowship. Gift and return, we might say, are simultaneous in the life of God, since the Father who gives to the Son in the Spirit is in the Son who returns the gift to the Father in the same Spirit. There is not even a moment of "stasis" or death, since "resurrection" life is offered back from the moment the original life is offered.

Yet, within the life of God we find the uncreated round of life and self-gift that is the original for the created pattern of death and resurrection. Even apart from the Fall, this pattern would be evident in the changes of seasons, the defoliating of trees and their springtime return, the dropping of petals from flowers and the vernal burst of new growth. Even in man, apart from the fall, the pattern of death and resurrection would be evident. For Adam it was not good to be alone, and so he went into a "deathlike" sleep, only to awaken to a greater, more glorious, more wonderful life than he could have conceived. Adam, the "original man," was incomplete without his supplement, but the supplement was not a degenerate form of the origin;

rather "the woman is the glory of the man" (1 Corinthians 11:7). And through the ages, apart from sin, humanity would have grown and would have been fitted out in garments of ever-increasing glory, eternally advancing in glory, and yet ever and always looking forward to an infinite advance yet to come. To suggest that the unfallen creation would have been free from this round and rhythm is to fall prey to the tragic metaphysics of ancient and modern philosophy, for it would imply that change, mutability, and becoming is a tragedy. But Scripture teaches that it is all "very good."

Death and resurrection, of course, is *the* comic theme, the comic theme of history, and there is thus a "comic" structure to the triune life, an eternal "story" of "emanation and remanation," of exile and return. Because this is the God who created and governs history, history manifests the same structure, and it is a story not of a golden age lost, nor even of a return to Edenic paradise, but a story in which the second moment, the final moment, is the glory of the first.

III.

Before examining how the Christian comic vision of history and reality affected Western literature, it will be useful to illustrate further how the problematics of supplementarity appear in Western thought. Especially it will be useful to indicate how supplementarity is a background issue in the various metaphysical problems discussed in the previous chapter.

Insofar as Western thought has been in anguish over the problem of "becoming," to that extent it has been in the grip of a false view of origin and supplement. Movement, for instance, is a kind of becoming, a change from one state of being to another, and can be conceived as a kind of supplementation. Originally, I am in one place, but then I "add" to my "being" in a single location a movement that takes me to another location. Moreover, if movement is supplementation, then so is time. It is 12:34 P.M. Or, it was when I began to write that sentence (several days ago now). Now that "moment of origin" has been added to, supplemented by the following seconds and minutes and days. Similarly, in metaphysical schemes such as Neoplatonism, all things that visibly exist are emanations from the "One," to which all things will eventually return. Thus everything that exists in the visible world has the character of supplement. Desire is also bound up with the problem of supplementarity. Assuming that desire arises from lack, the logic goes like this: if I were complete in myself, I would desire nothing, since I would lack nothing. Desire is a sign of the insufficiency of the origin.

In all of these specific areas, the issue is whether the additional moment of time, or the "addition" of movement to my static body, or the "emanation" from the "One" necessarily cancels out or does violence to the "original" location or moment. Does 12:35 P.M. "kill" 12:34 P.M.? Or, less colorfully, what is the direction of that supplement? Does the emanation obscure and hide the One, or displace it? Is the formation of particular things from the One a tragedy? According to Derrida, for the Western philosophical tradition, the direction is always a decline, yet the Western tradition has also occasionally recognized that supplements are "always already" present. Suppose you are a Neoplatonist asking about the supplementation of the One by its emanations; well, you *are* one of those emanations, and so the very question assumes the supplement. A Neoplatonist cannot inquire into a pure One because he exists as a contaminating supplement to the One. And by the time I say "12:35 P.M.," it is no longer so, since time has "always already" been supplemented. There is always already "supplement to the origin," and that is a problem that Western metaphysics, in Derrida's view, has not solved. And the "tragic" view that supplementation is always a "contamination" and a "diminishment" of the origin is a root assumption of the tragic metaphysics examined in the previous chapter.

Thus, a trinitarian affirmation of "supplement at the origin," and specifically of an *undiluted* supplement at the origin, gives us the tools to address the problems of time, creation, change, nature/law, and order/chaos that we have explored. A trinitarian theology is entirely capable of affirming the "always-already" aporias that postmodernism puzzles over. In the following pages, I briefly examine two modern issues in modern thought whose tragic conception of society and civilization manifest problems of supplementarity that a trinitarian theology unravels: first, briefly, the clash of desire and social convention, and, second, the clash of nature and culture.

Discontents of Civilization

In a number of respects, Freud, one of the grand theorists of modernity, displayed a profoundly tragic sensibility. This was particularly evident in his account of how desire clashes with social morals. Contrary to popular opinion, Freud was no amoralist, but rather, as Philip Rieff argued, possessed the "mind of a moralist." His morality, to be sure, was not Christian morality, but he was not an advocate of free sexuality (though he thought "Victorian" sexual morals too restrictive). He recognized that desire, associated in some phases of his work with the id, was impossible of fulfillment. One simply cannot fulfill every one of his desires without descending into bestiality. Id-fulfillment and civilization are simply incompatible. Civilization is necessary to human existence, yet it comes at the price of a tragic frustration of desire. Human life is locked in a no-win clash between desire and social demand, and the best that can be hoped is a kind of Stoic negotiation of this clash, which Freud associated with a well-adjusted ego.

In almost Freudian terms, Nathaniel Hawthorne explored the inherently tragic struggled of desire and civilization in various novels, perhaps most thoroughly in *The Scarlet Letter*. The first mark of civilization, Hawthorne says in the opening chapter, is the black rose of the prison door; if civilization is to function at all, there must be chains and shackles. The rose outside the prison door, which sprang from the ground where Anne Hutchinson strode, is a sign of the vitality that might exist within the city, but the city itself is defined by the black rose of control, law, and suppression of desire. Within this situation, Hester and Dimmesdale's love cannot be fulfilled. They experience a brief moment of happiness only when they leave the city for a brief respite in the forest, in a natural world where no black roses bloom. But Hawthorne does not leave his hero and heroine in the forest. He knows that they must come back to face the consequences of their actions, to face the certain prospect of death. Desire is frustrated, but this is the cost of civilized social life. Man is not a forest creature, though, tragically, he has a bit of the forest within him. Man cannot live as a "pure" natural man, and so there is a necessary supplement to nature; but at the same time, this supplement forces man into tragic choices and painful suppression of desire. Social conventions are humanly constructed and are not of the "original" nature of man. Yet, they are essential to human life. The supplement of natural desire by social convention is unavoidable, a necessary "supplement at the origin," but an essentially tragic supplement.

Meum *and* Tuum

In another sense, Rousseau's vision of human society is equally tragic. Though Rousseau, reversing the introspective penitence of Augustine's *Confessions*, wrote a *Confessions* without remorse about a being without original sin, his apparently comic outlook masks the tragic vision of human life and society that Rousseau develops. Derrida, whose work we shall examine in the following chapter, develops his concept of "supplementarity" in the course of a discussion of Rousseau. As noted above, he points out that for Rousseau, nature is the full origin, the plenitude of being, but notes that Rousseau also admits that Nature is sometimes insufficient. One cannot be a child of nature without also supplementing nature.

This same pattern applies to Rousseau's notion of the social contract, as developed in *The Origins of Inequality*. According to Rousseau, man was originally in a blissful and asocial state of nature. But nature requires the supplementation of society and culture, because there are threats to man in his natural state that cannot be met alone.

In proportion as the human race grew more numerous, men's cares increased. The difference of soils, climate and seasons, must have introduced some differences in their manner of living. Barren years,

long and short winters, scorching summers which parched the fruits
of the earth, must have demanded a new industry. On the shore and
the banks of rivers, they invented the hook and line, and became
fishermen and eaters of fish. In the forests they made bows and arrows, and became hunters and warriors. In cold countries they
clothed themselves with the skins of the beasts they had slain. The
lightning, a volcano, or some lucky chance acquainted them with fire,
a new resource against the rigours of winter: they learned how to
preserve this element, then how to reproduce it, and finally how to
prepare with it the flesh of animals which before they had eaten raw.[8]

Gradually, men came to realize that the way to achieve best advantage was to supplement nature with associations, however minimal,
of society.

Taught by experience that the love of well-being is the sole motive
of human actions, he found himself in a position to distinguish the
few cases in which mutual interest might justify him in relying upon
the assistance of his fellows; and also the still fewer cases in which a
conflict of interests might give cause to suspect them. In the former
case, he joined in the same herd with them, or at most in some kind
of loose association, that laid no restraint on its members, and lasted
no longer than the transitory occasion that formed it. In the latter
case, every one sought his own private advantage, either by open
force, if he thought himself strong enough, or by address and cunning, if he felt himself the weaker.

Once man begins to gather into societies, however, the distinction
of *meum* and *tuum* is immediately introduced. And this distinction is
the source of all the evils of human society.

The first man who, having enclosed a piece of ground, bethought
himself of saying "This is mine," and found people simple enough to
believe him, was the real founder of civil society. Humanity would
have been spared infinite crimes, wars, homicides, murders, if only

[8]Translated by G. D. H. Cole, available at http://www.constitution.org/jjr/ineq.htm.

someone had ripped up the fences or filled in the ditches and said, "Do not listen to this pretender! You are eternally lost if you do not remember that the fruits of the earth are everyone's property and that the land is no-one's property!" But by that point things had changed so drastically that there was no turning back, for this idea of "property," which develops out of prior ideas, did not form spontaneously in the human mind. Men had to progress, acquiring knowledge and arts, transmitting and increasing these from generation to generation, before they reached the last stage in the natural human state.

Rousseau wants to posit a natural man, without society, economy, or culture. But he realizes that nature is insufficient of itself, and therefore requires the supplement of culture. This is a necessary supplement to fill in the gaps of nature, but it is also a tragic supplement, because it leads to all the evils of actual human societies. A trinitarian theology can make sense of the always-already of nature and culture: nature is always already "added to" by culture. There is, in fact, no natural reality that can be distilled and isolated from cultural forms. Sexual desire is "natural," we think, but in all sorts of ways sexual desire has been formed and shaped by the sexual practices and rules of our culture. A trinitarian theology can make sense of the reality of Genesis 2: God created Adam, a "natural" man if ever there was one, and placed him immediately in a "garden," a cultural construct if there ever was one. Adam was not, even for a moment, an a-cultural being. His "nature" was to be "cultural." This always-already of nature and culture reflects the always-already of the divine society. It is just what we would expect from a world created by a God who is always already Father and Son and Spirit.

III
Tragic Literature

5

Ancient Literature and Tragedy

Nᴏᴛ ꜱᴜʀᴘʀɪꜱɪɴɢʟʏ, given the tragic conception of history and of metaphysics found in Greek culture, Greek literature is dominated by tragedy, tragedy here understood in its "Chaucerian" sense as a story with an unhappy ending. This is not to say that a Christian sort of tragedy is impossible, nor that the Greeks produced no comedies. Christian writers like Shakespeare and Dostoevsky wrote profound "tragedies" in a Christian mode, and Greeks like Aristophanes produced comedies. Nor am I suggesting that ancient comedy wholly lacked elements of rebirth or regeneration, of eschatology. There is often a new order of things at the end of many of the comedies: the birds wrest authority from the gods, Socrates' "Thinkery" is burned to the ground, and so forth. Yet, there is in Greek literature generally a bias toward tragedy and an inability to arrive at what I will call "deep comedy."

Even when Greeks wrote comedy, as W. H. Auden pointed out, it differs markedly from Christian comedy:

> Comedy is not only possible within a Christian society, but capable of much greater breadth and depth than classical comedy. Greater in breadth because classical comedy is based on a division of mankind into two classes, those who have *arete* [heroic virtue] and those who do not, and only the second class, the fools, shameless rascals, slaves, are fit subjects for comedy. But Christian comedy is based

upon the belief that all men are sinners; no one, therefore, whatever his rank or talents, can claim immunity from the comic exposure and, indeed, the more virtuous, in the Greek sense, a man is,
the more he realizes that he deserves to be exposed. Greater in depth
because, while classical comedy believes that rascals should get the
drubbing they deserve, Christian comedy believes that we are for-
bidden to judge others and that it is our duty to forgive each other.
In classical comedy the characters are exposed and punished: when
the curtain falls, the audience is laughing and those on stage are in
tears. In Christian comedy the characters are exposed and forgiven:
when the curtain falls, the audience and the characters are laughing
together.

Greek (and other classical) comedy evokes laughter *at* someone
who has suffered disaster. Homer's warriors get a big kick out of the
pummeling of Theophrastus, and they have a hearty laugh when little
Ajax slips into a pile of dung in Book 23 of the Iliad. Even the gods
laugh most riotously when they are able to catch Mars and Venus *in
flagrante delicto*. Christian laughter, in contrast, is laughter *with*.

Ancient literature, nonetheless, is marked as the literature of death
particularly in its bias toward tragedy. William Butler Yeats was not
your average orthodox Christian, but he recognized that a thresh-
old had been crossed with the coming of Christianity:

> Classical culture . . . was essentially a heroic culture, aristocratic and
> violent, its central myth the story of Oedipus, who kills his father
> and lives in incest with his mother. It was succeeded by Christian
> culture, which is democratic and altruistic, based on the myth of
> Christ, who appeases and reconciles his father, crowns his virginal
> mother, and rescues his bride the Church. . . . Tragedy is at the heart
> of Classical civilization, comedy at the heart of the Christian one.

Classical literature evokes no sense of "deep comedy," no confidence
that the world and history are fundamentally and profoundly good
and under the government of an unthinkably good God, no belief
that, in the words of St. Julian of Norwich (echoed by T. S. Eliot),

"all will be well and all manner of thing will be well." Deep comedy is a product of Christianity, a mark of resurrection life on the pages of Western literature.

Some ancient texts, of course, contain elements that come near to deep comedy. This chapter examines two of those: Homer's *Odyssey* and Virgil's *Aeneid*. In each case, however, we will find that death overshadows the final comedy of the epic conclusion—that even these most comic of classical works finally fail to attain deep comedy.

I.

As George Steiner has pointed out, the *Iliad* is the tragic epic of Greece, the source of the Greek tragic spirit and the source also of many of plots of tragic drama. The *Odyssey* is the comic masterpiece. This is evident from the overall structure of the epic, which is the story of a *nostos* or home-coming, of the rescue of Odysseus' bride, Penelope, and of justice dealt out to unruly suitors. The epic has an almost evangelical feel to it: Odysseus, the disguised king, returns to his homeland, is despised and rejected of men, but eventually triumphs over his enemies and secures his bride. Though there are threats in the *Odyssey*, death does not loom so near nor so fearfully as in the *Iliad*. In fact, Odysseus conquers death: though widely believed to be dead, he reappears, and at the center of the epic he travels through the underworld and returns. He is being bled white by the suitors, but rises again to shed *their* blood.

In many details, too, the theme of regeneration is apparent. At the beginning of the epic, Odysseus is found at the "navel of the sea," a womb image that indicates he is hidden away on Calypso's island awaiting rebirth. He emerges newborn from the sea on the island of Scheria, where he meets the Phaeacians, and when he arrives in Ithaca, he goes into a "death-like" sleep and then rises from it. There is a life-affirming thrust that is absent from the *Iliad* with its terrible wartime pressures; there is a delight in hearth and home and children, in living a normal life of a king, with wife and son and surrounded by his people. Odysseus is nothing so much as a homebody.

All this is the domestic stuff and context of comedy.[1] The symbolic geography of the epic underscores these comic elements. Odysseus journeys from the fantasy and horror-film world of "no man's land," where he braves the dangers of the chaotic sea, through the transitional/liminal world of the Phaeacians, to Ithaca, to his home, and finally to his bedroom. At the center of his world is the great bed, one of the posts of which is a live olive tree. This is the *umbilicus mundi*, the navel of the world, where he is reborn as a man settled on the land. He moves from the "navel of the sea" to the "navel of the earth," the domestic yet sacred pole around which his world is organized.

In large measure, this movement is a symbolic restoration to humanity, a point underscored by Homer's epic similes. When Odysseus first arrives at Scheria, the island of the Phaeacians, he is described with an epic simile as a lion. Having concluded that Nausikaa and her friends are harmless, he emerges from the leaves he has used as a bed:

> . . . great Odysseus crept out of the bushes.
> stripping off with his massive hand a leafy branch
> from the tangled olive growth to shield his body,
> hide his private parts. And out he stalked
> as a mountain lion exultant in his power
> strides through wind and rain and his eyes blaze
> and he charges sheep or oxen or chases wild deer
> but his hunger drives him on to go for flocks,
> even to raid the best-defended homestead.
> So Odysseus moved out . . . . (172)[2]

When he awakes at Ithaca, on his own island, however, he is no longer bestial:

> As a man aches for his evening meal when all day long
> his brace of wine-dark oxen have dragged the bolted plowshare

---

[1] Erich Segal, *The Death of Comedy* (Cambridge, Mass.: Harvard, 2001), 11.

[2] All quotations are from the translation by Robert Fagles (Penguin, 1996). Because Fagles's lines do not match the Greek text, I have cited by page number only.

down a fallow field—how welcome the setting sun to him,
the going home to supper, yes, though his knees buckle,
struggling home at last. So welcome now to Odysseus
the setting light of day. (287)

Having become a predatory beast at Troy, Odysseus is slowly, deliberately, being formed into a man.

Yet, this comic structure is crossed by the fact that Odysseus' return to humanity is simultaneously and necessarily an embrace of
mortality. Odysseus' journey to the underworld highlights this. In a
sense, this episode encapsulates his entire journey, since he is constantly threatened with death or at least with the prospect of never
regaining the life he once had in Ithaca. The fact that he emerges again
from the encounter with the dead is a sign that he triumphs heroically over death. Yet, while in the realm of the dead he receives guidance from Tiresias, who indicates that Odysseus cannot expect his
"triumph" over death to be permanent:

Once you have killed those suitors in your halls—
by stealth or in open fight with slashing bronze—
go forth once more, you must . . .
carry your well-planed oar until you come
to a race of people who know nothing of the sea,
whose food is never seasoned with salt, strangers all
to ships with their crimson prows and long slim oars,
wings that make ships fly. . . .
When another traveler falls in with you and calls
that weight across your shoulder a fan to winnow grain,
then plant your bladed, balanced oar in the earth
and sacrifice fine beasts to the lord god of the sea,
Poseidon. . . .
And at last your own death will steal upon you. . .
a gentle, painless death, far from the sea it comes
to take you down, borne down with the years in ripe old age
with all your people there in blessed peace around you. (253)

Odysseus does go through the realm of the dead and return, but his return is a return to a life that ends in death.

Odysseus' is a journey to death; it is also, explicitly, a journey *away from* immortality. Odysseus refuses Calypso's offer of immortality, choosing to remain human rather than share in the immortal life of the gods. Spurned, Calypso cannot understand Odysseus:

> "So then,
> royal son of Laertes, Odysseus, man of exploits,
> still eager to leave at once and hurry back
> to your own home, your beloved native land?
> Good luck to you, even so. Farewell!
> But if you only knew, down deep, what pains
> are fated to fill your cup, before you reach that shore,
> you'd stay right here, preside in our house with me
> and be immortal. Much as you long to see your wife,
> the one you pine for all your days . . . and yet
> I just might claim to be nothing less than she,
> neither in face nor figure. Hardly right, is it,
> for mortal woman to rival immortal goddess?" (158–159)

Like the son in Proverbs, Odysseus must choose between two women, the mortal and the immortal, and that decision shapes his future. He deliberately chooses the mortal Penelope: "Look at my wise Penelope. She falls far short of you, your beauty, stature. She is mortal after all and you, you never age or die. . . . Nevertheless I long—I pine, all my days—to travel home and see the dawn of my return" (159). At his final meal on Calypso's island, he sits to the side eating bread, while Calypso shares ambrosia with Hermes (158). His mortal has not put on immortality. Odysseus' story moves in the opposite direction from that of the gospel—not from death to life, but from the possibility of eternal life toward the certainty of death. Notice too that the only way for Odysseus to escape death would be for him to renounce all that makes him a man—his kingdom, his bride, his son, his home. An immortal man is an impossibility; to be human means to be journeying toward death.

Mortality, furthermore, has little to recommend it, as Odysseus knows well. He might be promised a happy old age and a quiet death surrounded by troops of friends, but what comes after is horrific. Throughout the journey through Hades, Odysseus meets the dead whose lives and words manifest the terrors of their state. Elpenor, one of Odysseus' men, had died by falling off the roof of Circe's house, a freakish, foolish, accidental death with not the least wisp of glory about it. Agamemnon obsessively describes his pathetic death at a banquet at the hands of his wife and her suitor. Achilles died with a reputation as the best of the Achaeans, but he finds that death brings no pleasure and says he would prefer to be a slave to being in Hades. Ajax is still resentful of Odysseus for seizing Achilles' armor. And this is the future Odysseus has chosen over eternity in the arms of a beautiful goddess.

Death continues to dog Odysseus at his homecoming. Even before he has had a chance to share a night of reunion with his wife, he tells her about Tiresias's prophecy. "One more labor lies in store," he tells Penelope, before urging her toward the bed. Penelope is not in a hurry:

> "If it's bed you want," reserved Penelope replied,
> "it's bed you'll have, whenever the spirit moves,
> now that the gods have brought you home again
> to native land, your grand and gracious house.
> But since you've alluded to it,
> since a god has put it in your mind,
> please, tell me about this trial still to come.
> I'm bound to learn of it later, I am sure—
> what's the harm if I hear of it tonight?" (463–464)

Even at home in his fixed-post bed, Odysseus is overshadowed by death. This contributes to what Charles Segal has identified as "an undercurrent of death" that pervades the Odyssey, "a deep and sad expression, characteristically Homeric, of the mixed and limited nature of all human happiness, of the inevitable involvement of man, even after his most strenuously attained and hoped for success, in time, change, and death."[3]

Viewed from a greater distance, the final resolution of the epic looks perfectly comic. The man is back, the bride rescued, the suitors destroyed, and the king on his rightful throne. Order and peace are restored, and Athena's pronouncement of peace being nearly the final word of the text. Yet alongside the reminder of death that casts a shadow on his reunion with Penelope, there are several other features of the ending that leave a less than comic feeling. The celebration of his return and victory over the suitors is marred by threats from the outside world. Eurycleia is not permitted to rejoice fully, lest neighbors passing by begin to suspect what has happened (452). Even in victory, Odysseus remains ever the veiled and cunning hero, so that the apocalypse, the "unveiling," remains incomplete. Even the wedding feast is in part a ruse, celebrated to distract attention from the victory (459–460). There is certainly no universal comic ending, for the danger of rivals and the threat of vengeance remains. Even within the terms of the heroic world, Odysseus' end is not thoroughly comic, for his story of victory and vengeance is not told to the Ithacans in general, but is only announced to the dead (468–474). What kind of hero is it whose heroic deeds are celebrated only in Hades?

From these and other considerations, Fidel Fajardo-Acosta concludes in a monograph on the *Odyssey* that the story is a tragedy. Fajardo-Acosta points to the origin of Odysseus' name as an indicator of his tragic duality. He is a "sufferer" but also a "giver of pain," and his identity is bound up with causing trouble to other people. Moreover, there are a number of hints that he has bestial qualities. His initiation into manhood occurs during a battle with a boar, and he is described as being like the boar himself, and according to Fajardo-Acosta's reading, he never matures out of this bestial-heroic mentality and character. He raids the Cicones at the beginning of his

---

[3] Charles Segal, *Singers, Heroes, and Gods in the Odyssey: Myth and Poetics* (Ithaca: Cornell Univ. Press, 1994), 37–38.

journey without any strategic purpose, and he is later duly punished for this. At Circe's island, he is not, like his men, literally turned into a pig, but does get turned into a plaything for the nymph, another of her pets. Perhaps he is not turned into a pig because he always has been one. When he kills the suitors, he gloats over them like a lion, and he hacks off the head of Leodes, who appears to be innocent, in a frenzy of blood wrath. Telemachus has to restrain him to keep him from behaving like a wild animal.[4] Fajardo-Acosta's arguments seem overly subtle, but they do indicate something of the ambiguous character of Odysseus, and the ambivalent comedy of the *Odyssey*.

II.

In Roman literature, the *Aeneid* is the chief counter-example to my thesis that ancient literature tends toward the tragic. As already indicated in chapter 1, Virgil is the first and virtually the only ancient writer to claim that the "golden age" was about to dawn again, and he saw that dawning incarnated in the empire of Augustus Caesar. As Jove says to his daughter Venus in Book 1:

> From that comely line
> The Trojan Caesar comes, to circumscribe
> Empire with Ocean, fame with heaven's stars.
> Julius his name, from Iulus handed down:
> All tranquil shall you take him heavenward
> In time, laden with plunder of the East,
> And he with you shall be invoked in prayer.
> Wars at an end, harsh centuries then will soften
> Ancient Fides and Vesta, Quirinus
> With Brother Remus, will be lawgivers,
> And grim with iron frames, the Gates of War
> Will then be shut: inside, unhold Furor,
> Squatting on cruel weapons, hands enchained
> Behind him by a hundred links of bronze,

---

[4] Fidel Fajardo-Acosta, *The Hero's Failure in the Tragedy of Odysseus: A Revisionist Analysis* (Lewiston, N.Y.: Edwin Mellen, 1990).

Will grind his teeth and howl with bloodied mouth. (13–14)[5]

This *imperium sine fine* brought peace to a war-torn world, established justice, and tied up the gates of war forever. Or so Virgil would have us believe that he believes.

The *Aeneid*, however, does not arrive at "deep comedy" any more than the *Odyssey*. Throughout the epic, Virgil drops hints that the empire was established only through tragic but necessary means and choices. One hint of this comes from the structurally significant use of the word "*condere*." At the end of the proem, Virgil writes that the sufferings Aeneas endured indicate that "so hard and huge a task it was to found [*condere*] the Roman people" (4), and in the closing lines of the epic, the word appears again: Aeneas "sank [*condit*] his blade in fury in Turnus's chest" (402). The connection suggests that the "founding" of Rome takes place only upon the "burial" of the sword in the enemy's chest. Virgil senses that this is the city of Man, the city of Cain, founded on the death of his brother. More generally, along the way toward his destiny, Aeneas leaves destruction in his wake. Of all the costs of the establishment of Rome, none is so dear as Dido, Queen of Carthage. She is one of the most attractive and sympathetic characters in the epic, indeed in all literature—competent, thoroughly regal, passionate, and wise but for loving the Trojan stranger. And yet, in order to achieve his destiny, Aeneas must leave her to her doom. Of course, this is Virgil's personalization of the Punic Wars, and a reminder that Roman achieved greatness by destroying the great civilization of North Africa.

Exploring the account of Dido's death in Book 4 and its parallels with Aeneas's description of the fall of Troy in Book 2 shows how deep Dido's tragedy runs.[6] In Book 2, Aeneas tells the story of the

---

[5] All quotations from the Aeneid are taken from Robert Fitzgerald's translation (Everyman's Library, 1992). I will cite page numbers, not line numbers, throughout.

[6] Much of the following depends on the superb treatment of the Aeneid in J. William Hunt, *Forms of Glory: Structure and Sense in Virgil's Aeneid* (Carbondale, Ill.: Southern Illinois Univ. Press, 1973).

fall of Troy, referring specifically to the Greek deceiver Sinon, who pretended to be an outcast of the Greeks in order to convince the Trojans to accept the Trojan horse. When Laocoon tries to warn the Trojans, he is hauled off by sea snakes along with his boys. Then the burning of the city is described in detail, climaxing with the death of Priam and the subsequent fall of the city. Book 4 echoes a number of the images from Book 2. In the opening lines of Book 4, Dido is described as being consumed by a fire of lust that recalls the fires of burning Troy: "Unlucky Dido, burning, in her madness roamed the city, like a doe hit by an arrow shot from far away" (97–98). Book 4 ends with a funeral pyre and a city in mourning as if the city itself had fallen:

> Now through the shocked city
> Rumor went rioting, as wails and sobs
> With women's outcry echoed in the palace
> And heaven's high air gave back the beating din,
> As though all Carthage or old Tyre fell
> To storming enemies, and, out of hand,
> Flames billowed on the roofs of men and gods.
> Her sister heard and trembling, faint with terror,
> Lacerating her face, beating her breast,
> Ran through the crowd to call the dying queen. (120)

As Aeneas leaves Carthage, he looks back to see the flames of Dido's pyre, which make the city appear to be in flames:

> Cutting through waves blown dark by a chill wind
> Aeneas held his ships firmly on course
> For a midsea crossing. But he kept his eyes
> Upon the city far astern, now bright
> With poor Elissa's pyre. What caused that blaze
> Remained unknown to watchers out at sea,
> But what they knew of a great love profaned
> In anguish, and a desperate woman's nerve,
> Led every Trojan heart into foreboding. (125)

Carthage goes up in "virtual flames" and undergoes a "virtual fall" because Dido accepts a man into her city, a man whose clothes still smell of the flames of fallen Troy. Dido's welcome of Aeneas replays the tragedy of Priam's acceptance of Sinon. Aeneas has left Troy behind, but in a real sense brings Troy with him, and causes another great city to fall. In the *Aeneid* Carthage is imagined as an Eastern city, like Troy itself, a city of more than oriental splendor. Aeneas leaves Carthage in ruins, without its beautiful and very able queen to preside over it. To found New Troy, in short, Aeneas has to cause another Troy to fall.

Aeneas's role in the "fall" of Carthage is also indicated by the gifts he offers to Dido. Astonishingly, he brings her a robe and veil used by Helen at the time she sailed away with Paris! Several of his gifts are from Priam's daughters, who are also dead or captured by the Greeks. Adorned by Aeneas, Dido is dressed like Helen and like the doomed princesses of Troy. Insofar as dress is destiny, Dido is doomed as soon as she accepts these gifts. Further, though Aeneas tells his son Ascanius to fetch the gifts, it is actually Cupid in disguise as Ascanius who gives the gifts. The connection is very close: Cupid is going to wound Dido with the wound of love that is going to flame up in her heart, and this flame is going to end with her pyre. As he did with Helen, Cupid inflames Dido to set a city in flames. If Carthage is another Troy, Dido is in central respects a new Helen.

Images from Carthage are brought back into play in the final books of the *Aeneid* in connection with the death of Turnus. For example, Virgil uses a "bee" simile to link Latium and Carthage. At his first view of the humming busyness of Carthage, Aeneas is duly impressed:

> Here men were dredging harbors, there they laid
> The deep foundation of a theatre,
> And quarried massive pillars to enhance
> The future stage—as bees in early summer
> In sunlight in the flowering fields
> Hum at their work, and bring along the young
> Full-grown to beehood; as they cram their combs

With honey, brimming all the cells with nectar,
Or take newcomers' plunder, or like troops
Alerted, drive away the lazy drones,
And labor thrives and sweet thyme scents the honey. (19)

Latium is a hive disturbed:

Amid the townspeople
Panic and discord grew: some said the town
Should be unbarred, gates opened to the Dardans;
These would hale to the walls the king himself.
The rest ran to fetch arms and man the ramparts.
As when a shepherd, tracking bees, has found
Their hive in tufa, he fills up the cleft
With acrid smoke; inside, roused in alarm,
The bees clamber about their waxen quarters,
Buzzing loud and growing hot with rage
As black and reeking puffs invade their home,
And deep in rocky dark their hum resounds
While smoke goes up in the clear air. (389)

This is only one of a series of parallels between Latium and
Carthage, which highlight the fact that Aeneas again is "attacking" a
city, and symbolically yet another city in flames. New Troy rises
phoenixlike from the ashes of old Troy, but only after it has also threatened to reduce Carthage and Latium to ashes. If Aeneas is the true
"Achilles" figure of the second part of Virgil's epic, the message is
even more strongly underlined: like the first Achilles, the Roman
Aeneas triumphs over a "Hector" (Turnus) and destroys his city and
civilization. To be sure, the Roman Achilles destroys it to make a new
city, but Virgil is quite taken by the destruction itself.

Structurally, as William Hunt argues, the *Aeneid* can be seen as a
triptych, its three "panels" formed by books 1–4, 5–8, and 9–12. The
first panel climaxes with the fire of Dido's pyre, while the final panel
ends with the death of Turnus. Both deaths are associated with imagery that suggests the fall and burning of a city. These side panels

are similar in structure, since both are themselves triptychs. Books 1–4 begin with Aeneas arriving in Carthage and meeting Dido, and end with Dido's death, the middle panel being Aeneas's description of the fall of Troy:

> Aeneas arrives in Carthage, Book 1
> Aeneas describes fall of Troy and journey, Books 2–3
> Dido's death and Aeneas's departure, Book 4

Similarly, Books 9–12 move from the introduction to Turnus to the death of Turnus, with the deaths of Nisus, Euryalus, and Camilla in the central panel:

> Aeneas arrives in Italy, Book 9
> Battle for Italy, Books 10–11
> Turnus's death and Aeneas's victory, Book 12

The structure of the two side triptychs is matched by the structure of the epic as a whole: the first third and the last third surround the story of the events that bring Aeneas to Italy, and the central panel climaxes with the revelation of the shield of Aeneas, which represents his triumph and the glory of Rome:

> Books 1–4: Aeneas in Carthage (death of Dido)
> Books 5–8: Aeneas journeys to Italy
> Books 9–12: Aeneas triumphs in Italy (death of Turnus)

Overall, the triptych consists of a side panel showing Dido's funeral pyre, and the sword in Dido's breast, and a side panel showing Aeneas burying his sword in Turnus's breast. In the middle stands mighty, *pius* Aeneas with his great shield.

Thus, though the *Aeneid* is a triumphant epic in many ways and though Aeneas is successful in many respects, there is still a tragic quality to the founding that is undeniable. This is not the tragic wisdom of Greek heroism, the recognition that the hero's life is short and therefore requires heroic deeds. Virgil's is a thoroughly Roman, which is to say, a political sort of tragedy, the tragic wisdom that the great founding events of Rome come at considerable cost. Peace comes at the cost of horrific destruction and tragic loss. These hints have led more than one commentator to conclude that Aeneas learns about the tragic quality of life. Lilian Feder writes that

> Aeneas pays a heavier price for his achievements than long toil and the weariness of battle; his task is accomplished only after he has learned the essential tragedy of all human experience, after he has accepted the paradox that great hopes are weighed down with painful responsibilities and that great achievements are qualified by the remembrance and eternal suggestion of human limitation. The poem is a story of success, but also of what one must pay for success. The painful mystery of tragic waste and shame and inevitable dissatisfaction intensifies the difficulty of achievement and sets it in relief against the background of all human experience.

And again,

> The cause is noble, but by inspiring violence and destruction it involves a tragic waste of noble spirits sacrificed to the cause. Aeneas is forever cast in a double role: the Roman leader fulfilling at any cost his obligation to his nation, and the man enduring pity and despair at every moment of victory. His acceptance of a knowledge of sorrow is both the cost and the gain of his accomplishment, and the task accomplished is what gives deliverance from and at the same time significance to the torment of those who failed.[7]

Viewing the carvings of the Trojan War on the walls of Juno's temple in Carthage, Aeneas comments "*sunt lacrimae rerum*," literally, "here are the tears of things" or, in Fitzgerald's translation, "they weep here for how the world goes." As noted in an earlier chapter, this is virtually a motto for Virgil. His final picture of the Roman hero is

---

[7] Qtd. in Hunt, *Forms of Glory*, 13.

that of a victor, faithful to his destiny, but a hero who is in tears at the moment of his triumph.

Given that every city we see in this epic meets with disaster, it is difficult to see how Virgil could avoid questioning the future of Rome. Even Book 6's grand scene of the future of Rome ends on a sour note, with the pathetic death of Marcellus. Virgil calls Rome the "*imperium sine fine*," but he seems more than a little aware of the fact that there is no such thing: that all *imperia* come to an end. Taken as he is with the falls of Troy, Carthage, and Latium, he seems more than a little aware that Romans will not live "happily ever after." He is more than a little infused with the tragic sensibility of ancient man.

III.

These epics are as close as ancient literature comes to "deep comedy." But the difference between the odyssey of Jesus and that of Odysseus could not be greater: Jesus, like Odysseus, goes through death and emerges on the far side, but Jesus emerges "never again to die," having put off the mortal flesh for immortal Spirit. Odysseus undergoes death in order to be "resurrected" only to mortality. That is as happy as it gets in ancient epic. Likewise, the difference between the tearful vision of peace and order in Virgil and the tearless promise of Revelation 21 is equally stark. Virgil lived to see a world at peace, but he cannot imagine a peace that does not come at the cost of destruction; he cannot imagine a peace other than the peace of the city of Cain, built on the blood of a brother. To gain a glimpse of deep comedy in literature, we must turn to Christian literature.

6

Deep Comedy

DEEP COMEDY, as I've argued, is a specifically Christian phenomenon rooted in the Christian gospel as the revelation of the triune character of God. It has profound—and in many respects still untapped—implications for an understanding of history and metaphysics. Below, I examine some features of medieval literature that show traces of resurrection and trinitarian comedy on the pages of literature. Deep comedy might also be explored in medieval art and architecture (nothing is more deeply comic than the farcical depiction of demons and monsters as gargoyles on medieval cathedrals), and it would be interesting to trace it in musical styles of the medieval and early modern worlds. To keep the discussion somewhat controlled and to stay somewhat within the limits of my competence, I have limited the discussion to literature. After examining some key themes in medieval literature, I turn to Shakespeare as the crowning illustration of the "deep comedy" of Christian literature.

I.

Your average textbook will tell you that medieval civilization was a dismal affair. Sober, serious, celibate churchmen gained control of the levers of power and ensured that everyone remained quite unhappy. As with many caricatures, this has some basis in fact. Benedict discouraged laughter in monasteries, and many clergy and theologians were suspicious of pleasure. In many ways, however, this is a

115

highly misleading picture. For one thing, when medieval writers wrote about tragedy, they explained that it was an ancient genre, no longer used. For the better part of a millennium, tragic drama and tragic story-telling virtually disappeared from medieval Europe, until revived by Chaucer and later more vigorously in the Renaissance.[1]

As the Russian literary critic Mikhail Bakhtin has shown, furthermore, alongside the serious "official" culture, there was a comic and farcical folk culture, which frequently invaded high culture. Bakhtin comments, for example, on the "school festivals, which played a large role in the cultural and literary life of the Middle Ages." At these events, monastic novices or university students "ridiculed with a clear conscience during the festival everything that had been the subject of reverent study during the course of the year—everything from Sacred Writ to his school grammar." Comedy made its appearance at other festivals as well. As Bakhtin writes,

> Medieval laughter is holiday laughter. The parodic-travestying "Holiday of Fools" and "Holiday of the Ass" are well known, and were even celebrated in the churches themselves by the lower clergy. Highly characteristic of this tendency is *risus paschalis*, or paschal laughter. During the paschal days laughter was traditionally permitted in church. The preacher permitted himself risqué jokes and gay-hearted anecdotes from the church pulpit in order to encourage laughter in the congregation—this was conceived as a cheerful rebirth after days of melancholy and fasting. No less productive was "Christmas laughter" (*risus natalis*); as distinct from the *risus paschalis* it expressed itself not in stories but in songs. Serious church hymns were sung to the tunes of street ditties and were thus given a new twist.[2]

Comedy was not seen as a dispensable addition to serious reflection, but almost as an independent mode of thought. According to

[1] See Henry Ansgar Kelly, *Ideas and Forms of Tragedy from Aristotle to the Middle Ages* (Cambridge: Cambridge Univ. Press, 1993).

[2] Bakhtin, *The Dialogic Imagination: Four Essays,* ed. Michael Holquist, trans. Caryl Emerson and Michael Holquist (Austin: Univ. of Texas Press, 1981), 72–73.

Bakhtin, Renaissance figures like Shakespeare, Cervantes, and Rabelais displayed a sense that comedy alone was capable of penetrating some of the secrets of the universe. For the Renaissance, "Laughter has a deep philosophical meaning; it is one of the essential forms of the truth concerning the world as a whole, concerning history and man; it is a peculiar point of view relative to the world; the world is seen anew, no less (and perhaps more) profoundly than when seen from the serious standpoint. . . . Certain essential aspects of the world are accessible only to laughter."[3] But these Renaissance insights were prepared by the comic literature and festival culture of the Middle Ages. Medieval satirists saw comedy everywhere: "Laughter was as universal as seriousness; it was directed at the whole world, at history, at all societies, at ideology. It was the world's second truth extended to everything and from which nothing is taken away. It was, as it were, the festive aspect of the whole world in all its elements, the second revelation of the world in play and laughter."[4]

Medieval laughter did not stand alone, but was reflected a larger medieval attitude toward death and evil. Bakhtin writes:

> It is the victory of laughter over fear that most impressed medieval man. It was not only a victory over mystic terror of God, but also a victory over the awe inspired by the forces of nature, and most of all over the oppression and guilt related to all that was consecrated and forbidden ("mana" and "taboo"). It was the defeat of divine and human power, of authoritarian commandments and prohibitions, of death and punishment after death, hell and all that is more terrifying than earth itself. . . . This feeling is expressed in a number of characteristic medieval comic images. We always find in them the defeat of fear presented in a droll and monstrous form, the symbols of power and violence turned inside out, the comic images of death and bodies rent asunder. All that was terrifying becomes grotesque.[5]

---

[3] *Rabelais and His World*, trans. Helene Iswolsky (Bloomington, Ind.: Univ. of Indiana Press, 1984), 66.

[4] Ibid., 84.

[5] Ibid., 90–91.

The high literature of the period is marked by these comic elements. Medieval writers loved to parody serious scholarly pursuits: "The Middle Ages produced a whole series of variants on the parodic-travestying Latin grammar. Case inflection, verbal forms and all grammatical categories in general were reinterpreted either in an indecent erotic context, in a context of eating and drunkenness or in a context ridiculing church and monastic principle of hierarchy and subordination." In one work, the so-called Virgilius Maro Grammaticus, the author invents quotations to illustrate grammatical points, cites fictitious authorities from ancient literature, and describes "a scholarly discussion lasting two weeks on the question of the vocative case of *ego*."[6] Even works that were not parodies have elements of laughter and comedy. Peter Hawkins has recently pointed out that the *Divine Comedy* is a comedy not only in the literary sense but in the common sense of the term—many passages of the *Comedy* are supposed to be *funny*. Medieval France produced farcical dramas, and even medieval plays on sacred themes, like the nativity drama known as *The Second Shepherds' Play,* included comic scenes and characters. Chaucer's penchant for bawdy humor was not unique to him.

Deep comedy involves not only laughter, but as Bakhtin recognized, a particular attitude toward the world. For ancient man, as we have seen, the world was sharply divided between chaos and order, and this was concretely and politically expressed in the division between the ordered cosmos of the city and the chaos of the world outside its walls. Socrates would rather drink his hemlock than suffer exile from Athens. Odysseus is the great adventurer of Greek legend, but his sole intention is to get home as quickly as possible, for beyond Ithaca, the world is populated by cyclopses, witches, monsters of the deep. Of course, ancient men were not motionless but traveled a great deal more than we give them credit for. But ancient man knew that every time he ventured outside the walls he was entering alien territory, into a world inhospitable to human life.

---

[6] *Dialogic Imagination,* 73.

During the high middle ages, particularly around the twelfth century, a new attitude toward the world begins to be reflected in the literature of romance. One of the key distinguishing marks of romance, as opposed to ancient and early medieval epic, is a new conception of "adventure," which is related to a different conception of the world. Two scholars in particular have paid attention to this feature of medieval literature and culture: Bakhtin and the German Marxist historian Michael Nerlich. Romance, Bakhtin points out, existed in antiquity. Yet, Bakhtin distinguishes between ancient romances of endurance, in which the character's goal was merely to stay constant through a series of adventures, and romances of transformation, in which the character is changed by his circumstances and the events of the story. Odysseus illustrates the first type of heroic adventurer, while the protagonist of Apuleius's *Golden Ass* illustrates the latter. Both sorts of romance, and both sorts of adventurers, however, share a key characteristic: according to Nerlich, "All figures of the Greek and Latin novels of adventure are 'involuntary' adventurers." Bakhtin too emphasizes that "an individual can be nothing other than completely passive, completely unchanging" and function as "merely the physical subject" of events. After the twelfth century, things changed, suddenly and permanently. In the Arthurian romances of Chrétien de Troyes and his legions of imitators, Nerlich says, "Adventures are undertaken on a *voluntary* basis, they are *sought out* (*la quete de l'aventure*, the quest for adventure), and this quest and hence the adventurer himself are glorified." Even the meaning of the term "adventure" changes: "*Aventure*, which in its literary occurrences before the courtly romance, means fate, chance, has become, in the knightly-courtly system of relations, an event that the knight must seek out and endure, although this event does continue to be unpredictable, a surprise of fate."[7]

This willingness to seek out adventure in the world outside one's home reflects a very changed attitude toward the world. Leaving the

---

[7] Nerlich, *Ideology of Adventure: Studies in Modern Consciousness, 1100–1750,* trans. Ruth Crowley (Minneapolis: Univ. of Minnesota Press, 1987).

confines of one's home and city loses all its terror, though it is still dangerous. To put it another way, the ancient distinction between the "normal" world of the home and city and the "magical" and "mysterious" world outside dissolves. Instead, the entire world has become normalized, every place seen as a place subject to God and filled with His presence. All places become "normalized." Or, one could see the reverse process at work: all places become infused with magic. As Bakhtin says, "The whole world becomes miraculous, so the miraculous becomes ordinary without ceasing at the same time to be miraculous . . . the entire world is subject to 'suddenly.'"[8]

Courtly heroes set out on adventures as much for the sake of their souls as for any good they might accomplish. Adventuring is essential to the development of character, or, in theological terms, to his sanctification. Nerlich says that "according to this ideology, the meaning of the knightly existence is the fulfillment of ethical principles in the experience of *aventures* and the demonstration of knightly virtues like bravery and loyalty to a revered lady, to the prince, or king and to God." For Erich Kohler, medieval adventure is "a self-testing with no specific task, with no office, with no concrete historical or political context." For these reasons, Nerlich is willing to go so far as to say that the modern mentality of adventure, travel, commercial "ventures," and so on can be traced back to the twelfth century and the works of Chrétien de Troyes. Chrétien was, he says, the first modern man.

Of course, many factors were at work in the development of the "adventuring" and "comic" viewpoint evident in medieval Christian literature, but it seems undeniable that Christianity itself was one of the key factors. Historical connections could be made stronger by exploring earlier Christian literature prior to the twelfth century. Adventure-seeking does not begin with Chrétien. Arguably, it begins with Paul and Acts, and comes to remarkable fruition in the lives of many of the early monks and missionaries of Christian history. Irish

---

[8] *Dialogic Imagination*, 73.

monks in particular, with their practice of White Martyrdom, are the precursors of the venturing knights of the high middle ages. Even Beowulf, though still operating in a more epic environment, goes to Hrothgar *seeking* to help. He is not a passive adventurer at the mercy of fate. He goes out looking for dangers to conquer. This outward movement is deeply rooted in biblical history. The postdiluvian history of God's people begins with Abraham, and he is simply a different kind of creature than had ever existed in literature before. Abraham's story begins with a call to leave his father's house and venture toward a land he has never seen by a route that has not been shown. Abraham is a different kind of human being from Socrates or Odysseus, and he engenders a different sort of people. Though Abraham might be cited as the source of the "adventuring" mentality, this was given an even stronger impetus by the Christian gospel. The Old Testament order in Israel was similar in many respects to the order of Ancient Near Eastern civilizations or Greece. In Israel as in Athens, the city and temple were seen at the center of the world. Everything moved centripetally toward the temple. Exile was the final and most severe curse of the Old Covenant.

At the heart of the gospel, however, is the announcement that this order of sacred center and profane distance has been destroyed. Instead of a single place for an early temple, the New Testament announces a heavenly temple, equally accessible from any point on earth. The commission of the Greater Joshua is not to enter the land in order to stay there; rather it is "Go, make disciples of all nations." The gospel further promotes the deep comedy of adventure because it declares that there is no chaos outside the city. Christ is Lord of all, and all things are, in principle, subdued to Him. Irish monks can be confident that wherever the sea might take them, they will still be in God's world and will meet human beings who need a Savior.

More directly, Christians worshiped a God whose crowning work was nothing less than a grand "adventure," a voluntary movement from the security of the triune fellowship into the alien and dangerous world of sinful human beings. Christians proclaimed an "advent" of God the Son, and it is no accident that there is an etymological connection between "advent" and "adventure." It is no accident that the people of an adventurous God should produce the adventurous literature of deep comedy.

II.

More could of course be said of the medieval achievement in literature, and perhaps someday I shall have a chance to return to it. But in English literature at least, deep comedy comes to its fullest expression in the comedies and tragedies of Shakespeare. Nothing shows the distance from ancient conceptions of reality so clearly as a comparison of Shakespeare's world with the worlds of ancient tragedy, epic, and drama. In order to keep the argument concrete, I examine below two of Shakespeare's plays, first *King Lear*, without doubt the most tragic of Shakespeare's tragedies, the other a comedy, *Twelfth Night*. In both of these, though in very different ways, the Christian comic vision of history and reality will be manifest.

Today, *King Lear* is widely considered Shakespeare's greatest tragedy and even his greatest achievement. Elements of the play that made it unpalatable to earlier generations are viewed as peculiar strengths by modern critics. Especially in the mid-twentieth century, when absurdist theater was in its heyday, *Lear* was seen as an important precursor. Though absurdism now looks positively quaint, critics commonly interpret the world of *Lear* as if it were Elizabethan absurdist theater. One critic concludes that the play is a "tragedy of penance" that takes place in an "imbecile universe" in which there is no hint of "charity, resiliency, or harmony." Another says that the play makes "it impossible to retain *any* concept of an ordered universe" and promotes "the reflection that any system of order results in very strange notions of justice." In his reading, the play directly challenges Christian notions of salvation: "In the end the subtlest and most tempting order of all is undone—the order of repentance, forgiveness, redemption and regeneration is reversed in unregenerate Lear's tottering broken-hearted into madness and death."

Critics seem to have strong grounds for taking Gloucester's comment as the play's theme: "As flies to wanton boys are we to the gods; they kill us for sport" (4.1.37–8). As some have pointed out, *Lear* never moves far from its first scene. It begins with Lear divesting himself of all the accouterments of kingship, renouncing his daughter Cordelia because she can say "nothing" to express her love for her father, and sending faithful Kent, who defends Cordelia, into exile. The play ends on the same note. Shortly before the final scenes, Lear impatiently drives Kent from his sight ("Prithee away") and weeps over his beloved Cordelia, who is again silent, this time in death. And, significantly, Lear dies calling out for someone to help him unbutton his robe (5.3.307). The wheel turns. The tide moves in, the tide moves out. Vanity of vanities, all is vanity.

In other respects the design of the play consistently raises hope only to frustrate it. Gloucester's son Edgar, disguised for his own protection as "Poor Tom," a homeless and insane wanderer, no sooner finishes saying "things could not get worse" than he sees his father tottering across the heath with blood-stained bandages on his vacant eyes (4.1.1–12). Near the end, Albany prays for Cordelia's safety; then, immediately, "Enter Lear with Cordelia in his arms," howling at the heavens (5.3.254f.). Every time we feel that things might at last turn around, our hopes are sadistically dashed.

Lear's use of comic conventions has similar effects. There are comic elements in Shakespeare's other great tragedies. *Hamlet* lurches toward farce at several points and has inspired zany off-shoots like Stoppard's *Rosencrantz and Guildenstern Are Dead*. Even austere *Macbeth* has its drunken porter. But no tragedy has so much in common with comedy as *Lear*. Spatially, the movement of the play is reminiscent of comedy. Peter Saccio has pointed out that Shakespearean comedies are often comedies of escape. Lovers (especially lovers) find city or home frustrating: its rules are obstacles to desire, its structures of authority are suffocating, its authority figures (notably fathers) are tyrants. The solution? Escape to the woods, to a pre-political and pre-social Eden where the difficulties of life can be set aside and where all can be renewed. *Lear* shares this structure with *A Midsummer Night's Dream*, *Cymbeline*, *The Tempest* and other comedies and romances. *King Lear* begins with a disordered world, where child stands against father and father against child, an apocalyptic world of blood, fire, and vapor of smoke. Lear and his small band of outcasts go out into the heath, a natural setting that, in a comedy, would be a place of regeneration. Instead of a brightly lit green world, they enter a stormy and nightmarish landscape. Their return to nature does not bring renewal to the social and political world, for the play ends as disastrously as it begins. We know from the comedies that Eden lies "outside" the walls of the human city. We learn from *Lear* that Hell is outside as well.

Lear's Fool, moreover, plays the role that fools normally do in Shakespearean comedy—to highlight the actual folly of the world by the wisdom that shines out from their pretended folly. *Lear* has a prominent fool because it is about the world as a "great stage of fools." Jokes that are funny in the drawing room of Illyria (*Twelfth Night*), however, echo ominously in the empty world of *Lear*. Shakespearean comedy (following the conventions of Roman New Comedy and anticipating P. G. Wodehouse) frequently arises from mistaken identities: two characters, often a master and servant, exchange clothes and names, and the play traces the comic confusion that ensues. Again, *Lear* is unique among the tragedies in the prominence of this device. To be sure, *Hamlet* is all about acting—Hamlet acting out an antic disposition, Claudius acting as if Denmark is safe and he is legitimately king, the players acting out the murder of Hamlet's father. But *Lear*'s characters actually adopt alternative identities. Hamlet playing mad Hamlet is still Hamlet. Kent becomes Caius, Edgar becomes Poor Tom and pretends to be a Dover fisherman after his father "falls" from the cliffs. In all these respects, Shakespeare teases us with comic conventions and raises expectations of a comic resolution, only to pull out the props from under us. The play is generically a tragedy, but these comic elements give it the feel of black comedy.

This thoroughgoing desolation is undoubtedly deliberate on Shakespeare's part. Holinshed's *Chronicle*, one of Shakespeare's main historical sources, recorded that Lear was in the end restored to power, with Cordelia alive and fully restored to his good graces. Of this comic ending, there is virtually nothing in Shakespeare's play. The horrifying parallel plot of Gloucester and his sons is likewise Shakespeare's own contribution to the story.

In an important sense, this pattern of frustrated optimism is a sign of the effect of deep comedy on tragic drama. The play is filled with the unrealized possibility of restoration, redemption, resurrection, in a way that an ancient tragedy could never be. Ancient tragedy took place in a world where resurrection was unknown, where death was the end, but the world of King Lear is potentially a far happier place. The fact that this potential is not realized enhances the feeling of waste.

But another aspect of deep comedy is perhaps more important to *Lear*. Simply put, Shakespeare's play takes place, for all the paganism of its character and its story, in a Christian universe. Occasional glimpses of Christian terminology and belief flash out from the darkness. Cordelia is said to redeem from the curse (4.5.202–3), and France speaks of her as being loved despite her forsakenness (1.1.251). Cordelia at one point says that she must be about her "father's business" (4.3.23–4). Edgar disguises himself as Poor Tom by sticking nails into his flesh (2.2.179).[9] More importantly, though the play is hardly poetically just, the distribution of punishments is not wholly random. Innocents (i.e., Cordelia) are engulfed in the tragedy, as innocents always are, but in the main the characters who die deserve death—Edmund, Gonerill, Regan, Oswald, and Cornwall. Characters who suffer despite their loyalty and love, particularly Kent and Edgar, are vindicated and live to tell the story. Cynical theological assessments from some characters are, moreover, challenged by other characters, and in one case a single character offers opposing views. Gloucester, as we have noted, delivers one of the bleakest comments

[9] Some productions enhance the christological symbolism by dressing Tom in a loin cloth and putting a crown of thorns on his head.

about the ways of the gods, yet following his "miraculous" survival after falling (so he believes) off the cliffs of Dover, he offers thanks to the "gentle gods" (4.5.215). To be sure, this incident highlights Gloucester's gullibility, but even when that is factored in, his theology has undergone a fundamental shift. Even if Gloucester were the only character, then, his statement about the malicious gods could not be taken simplistically as the play's theme. The nihilistic moments demand explanation, but they can be fully explained by a Christian reading of Shakespeare—or, rather, by reading Shakespeare as a Christian playwright, a playwright deeply imbued with the Christian comic vision of reality. For in *Lear* tragic outcomes do not occur because the world is designed for tragedy. Tragic outcomes occur because men sin.

This is established early in *Lear* in a conversation between the bastard Edmund and his father Gloucester. When Edmund falsely informs Gloucester that his legitimate son, Edgar, is conspiring against him, Gloucester claims that the treachery has been foretold in the stars:

> These late eclipses in the sun and moon portend no good to us. Though the wisdom of nature can reason it thus and thus, yet nature finds itself scourged by the sequent effects: love cools, friendship falls off, brothers divide. In cities, mutinies; in countries, discord; in palaces, treason; and the bond cracked 'twixt son and father. This villain of mine comes under the prediction: there's son against father; the king falls from bias of nature: there's father against child. Machinations, hollowness, treachery, and all ruinous discords follow us disquietly to our graves. (1.2.103–112)

The setting illustrates the horrors listed in the speech, for Gloucester is speaking to Edmund, the real treacherous son.

Edmund, however, will have none of it, for he knows that the problem is not in the stars but in ourselves. After listening to his father's ruminations on astrology, he soliloquizes on fate and free will:

This is the excellent foppery of the world, that when we are sick in
fortune—often the surfeits of our own behaviour—we make guilty
of our disasters the sun, the moon, the stars, as if we were villains
on necessity, fools by heavenly compulsion, knaves, thieves, and
treachers by spherical predominance, drunkards, liars, and adulter-
ers by an enforced obedience of planetary influence; and all that we
are evil in by a divine thrusting-on. An admirable evasion of whoremaster man, to lay his goatish disposition to the charge of a star.
(1.2.118–128)

That Edmund is himself of thoroughly goatish disposition, that he
is the epitome of whoremaster man, does not alter the orthodoxy
of his statement, which captures both the Christian notion of freedom and the Christian doctrine of original sin. These two points are
essential ground for any interpretation of *Lear*. The world is a "great
stage of fools," for sure; but it is so because man has chosen folly over
wisdom and loved darkness rather than light. Man is not evil by
"spherical predominance" or through a "divine thrusting-on." The
world of *Lear* is not designed to force anyone to do evil or trap them
in tragedy.

No passage in Shakespeare expresses this theme so well or so fully
as the speech of Ulysses from *Troilus and Cresida* 1.3. Ulysses is de-
scribing the effects of Agamemnon's foolish leadership of the Greek
warriors at Troy, and his analysis is so relevant to *King Lear* that it must
be quoted at more than polite length:

The specialty of rule hath been neglected;
And look how many Grecian tents do stand
Hollow upon this plain, so many hollow factions.
When that the general is not like the hive
To whom the foragers shall all repair,
What honey is expected? Degree being vizarded,
Th'unworthiest shows as fairly in the mask.
The heavens themselves, the planets, and this center
Observe degree, priority, and place,
Insisture, course, proportion, season, form,

Office, and custom, in all line of order.
And therefore is the glorious planet Sol
In noble eminence enthroned and sphered
Amidst the other, whose med'cinable eye
Corrects the ill aspects of planets evil
And posts, like the commandment of a king,
Sans check, to good and bad. But when the planets
In evil mixture to disorder wander,
What plagues and what portents, what mutiny,
What raging of the sea, shaking of the earth,
Commotion in the winds, frights, changes, horrors,
Divert and crack, rend and deracinate
The unity and married calm of states
Quite from their fixture! O, when degree is shaked,
Which is the ladder of all high designs,
The enterprise is sick. . . .

. . . .

Take but degree away, untune that string,
And hark what discord follows. Each thing meets
In mere oppugnancy. The bounded waters
Should lift their bosoms higher than the shores
And make a sop of all this solid globe;
Strength should be lord of imbecility,
And the rude son should strike his father dead;
Force should be right; or rather, right and wrong,
Between whose endless jar justice resides,
Should lose their names, and so should justice too.
Then everything includes itself in power;
Power into will, will into appetite;
And appetite, an universal wolf,
So doubly seconded with will and power,
Must make perforce an universal prey
And last eat up himself. (1.3.78–124)

The turmoil Ulysses describes is similar to the disorders of which
Gloucester complained. Ulysses' analysis of the causes is completely
different. His speech analyzes social and political chaos in terms of

what E. M. W. Tillyard called "the Elizabethan world picture." Ulysses would have recognized that the state of Lear's world—wolfish appetite devouring itself—was the result of "untuning" the string of degree. It was a result of an assault on the proper order of life.

Macbeth's famous "sound and fury" speech provides another perspective on *Lear*. Learning of his lady's death, Macbeth responds with utterly Stoic resignation:

> She should have died hereafter.
> There would have been time for such a word—
> Tomorrow, and tomorrow, and tomorrow,
> Creeps in this petty pace from day to day
> To the last syllable of recorded time;
> And all our yesterdays have lighted fools
> The way to dusty death. Out, out, brief candle!
> Life's but a walking shadow, a poor player,
> That struts and frets his hour upon the stage
> And then is heard no more. It is a tale
> Told by an idiot, full of sound and fury,
> Signifying nothing. (5.5.17–28)

This is as bleak a note as anything in *Lear*, but it is hardly the play's final word on the world. This is the speech of a man who has drenched himself in blood, who has waded so far into the river of slaughter that plunging on ahead has become far easier than repenting. The closing lines of the play could not offer a starker contrast: Malcolm, the legitimate king returned to Scotland, promises to do all that is necessary to restore his land "by the grace of Grace" (5.6.111). No doubt the world is absurd to Macbeth; but Macbeth has made it so.

These two passages are especially relevant to *Lear*. Ulysses' speech could almost be read as a summary of *Lear*, beginning with the untuning of the string of degree and ending in (nearly) universal carnage. Lear, moreover, is another Macbeth, or, better, he is Duncan and Macbeth rolled into one—both king and regicide. He is Adam, and his "original sin" makes his world a bleak and hopeless place.

Lear makes the world meaningless first of all for himself. This dynamic is evident from the opening scene of the play, in which Lear divests himself of all responsibility for rule, retaining the title of king but none of the duties. He intends to "divide in three our kingdom" in order to "shake all cares and business from our age," while he "unburdened crawls toward death" (1.1.37–41). From the moment that Lear removes his crown and kingship, he starts down a path that leads toward "nothing," a key word in the opening scene. When Lear demands that Cordelia express her love for him, she has "nothing" to say, and the exchange between Cordelia and Lear hammers the point home:

> *Cordelia*: Nothing, my lord.
> *Lear*: Nothing?
> *Cordelia*: Nothing.
> *Lear*: Nothing will come of nothing. Speak again. (1.1.86–90)

Like the repetition of "murder" when Hamlet meets his father's ghost, this repetition establishes a leitmotif that runs through the opening scenes.

Though Lear claims that Cordelia will receive nothing for saying nothing, in fact "nothing will come of nothing" more accurately describes his own future. Cordelia finds a true lover in the King of France, who considers her "most rich, being poor, most choice, forsaken, and most loved, despised" (1.1.250–251). For France, Cordelia's honesty and beauty are sufficient dowery. She is given all she needs. Something *did* come from her "Nothing." But the king who *gives* nothing, the king who wants *only* to receive, ends with nothing. Nothing comes from his "Nothing." Lear voluntarily deprives himself of all authority to rule, and his favored daughters Gonerill and Regan progressively deprive him of soldiers, servants, and finally shelter and sanity.

This stripping of Lear comes to a telling climax in an exchange with Regan and Gonerill, who are debating how many servants and soldiers Lear needs in his entourage. Regan insists that he cannot come to her house with more than twenty-five, and Lear appeals to Gonerill for more favorable treatment:

> *Gonerill*: Hear me, my lord;
> What need you five-and-twenty, ten, or five
> To follow, in a house where twice so many
> Have a command to tend you?
> *Regan*: What need one? (2.4.254–258)

Anguished, Lear cries "O, reason not the need!" If man is allowed no more than he *needs*, "man's life is cheap as beast's" (2.4.259–262). Exactly so. Lear's needs have been "reasoned" out, and a moment later, Lear is driven from the house and sent into the outer darkness. Eventually he sheds his last ragged pieces of clothing. He is reduced to "nothing" but his essential, bestial self.

Lear is not only deprived of all accommodations of civilized man, but also removed from all fellowship and communion. Again (like Macbeth) this outcome is a direct result of his own actions, his abdication. He fails to discern the true feelings of Regan and Gonerill, just as he misreads the genuine love behind Cordelia's "nothing." As a result, he pushes away the only ones who are truly loyal to him, the two members of his court who tell him the truth—Cordelia and Kent—and associates himself instead with treachers.

The tragedy, of course, is not Lear's alone. He discovers that nothing comes from nothing, and learns that beneath all the clothing and trappings "unaccommodated man" is nothing more than "a poor, bare, forked animal" (3.4.103–105). But the fact that the *king* comes to nothing means that the kingdom too descends into the void. These two dimensions to the play are directly connected, and both arise from Lear's original sin. When he gives up his throne and crown, Lear expresses the hope that this early peaceful division of the kingdom will prevent future violent division (1.143–45). In fact, his divestiture makes conflict inevitable: "Untune that string and see what discord follows." Without a tamer on the throne, beasts are unleashed and the righteous go into hiding in caves and hovels. The disorder that

Gloucester foresaw actually happens, not because of the stars but because of Lear's folly.

In a sense, this result is exactly the result that Lear had asked for. When Cordelia refuses to flatter him, he rejects her with terrible curses, abdicating as a father even as he has abdicated as a king:

> Here I disclaim all my paternal care,
> Propinquity and property of blood,
> And as a stranger to my heart and me
> Hold thee from this for ever. The barbarous Scythian,
> Or he that makes his generation messes
> To gorge his appetite, shall to my bosom
> Be as well neighboured, pitied, and relieved
> As thou my sometime daughter. (1.1.113–119)

Lear believes that Cordelia is the barbarian who "makes his generations messes," feeding on the father who had given her all. In fact, he is throwing himself at the mercy of Scythians, Regan and Gonerill, who gorge their appetites on their father's wealth, who "digest" portions of his kingdom (1.1.93–94), who prove themselves "pelican daughters" (3.4.76–77). Animal imagery clusters around Gonerill in particular. She is a kite, wolf, boar, and tiger, and her own husband says that in her world "humanity must perforce prey on itself/ Like monsters of the deep" (4.3.49–50). We find echoes of Ulysses' speech once again.

Appetite for power is joined to run-of-the-mill and rather tawdry sexual lust. Gonerill and Regan, partners in reducing Lear to nothing, become rivals for the love of Edmund, who plays both of them like a master musician. Edmund's rise to prominence depends partly on his skill in playing to the sisters' lusts. In the fallen world after Lear's withdrawal, it is fitting that Edmund, the bastard child of appetite who is wholly governed by goatish appetites, should worm his way to prominence. The social and political results of Lear's abdication come to fullest expression in Act 3, whose structure underlines the fact that bestiality and barbarity rule the kingdom. Scenes on the heath focusing on Lear and his company alternate with scenes of the court focusing on Edmund, Cornwall, and Regan. On the surface, it appears that the "community" on the heath is the community of beasts and barbarians; they are, after all, unaccommodated with house or clothing. But the scene's structure makes it clear that the real barbarism is elsewhere. A world of fools and madmen is more humane than the world of the sane. Though the men on the heath are stripped of all the "lendings" of nature and become utterly unaccommodated, they are merely exposing to view what is true beneath the finery of the court. On the heath, Kent and others help Lear find shelter, and they even give assistance to Poor Tom (Edgar) when they mistakenly invade his shelter. Meanwhile, the "civilized" world is a house of horrors. Edmund plots against his father (3.3), treacherously accusing him of being a traitor and finally receiving his father's title as a reward (3.5). In the last scene in the court, Cornwall and Regan savagely torture Gloucester and pluck out his eyes, while Cornwall is fatally wounded in the scuffle (3.7). Are these people really the civilized ones?

Lear captures the point precisely:

> . . . a dog's obeyed in office.
> Thou rascal beadle, hold thy bloody hand.
> Why dost thou lash that whore? Strip thy own back.
> Thou hotly lusts to use her in that kind
> For which thou whipp'st her. The usurer hangs the cozener.
> Through tattered clothings great vices do appear;
> Robes and furred gowns hide all. Plate sins with gold,
> And the strong lance of justice hurtless breaks;
> Arm it in rags, a pygmy's straw does pierce it. (4.6.159–168)

Though this passage might be taken as support for an absurdist interpretation, it is far more compatible with a Christian reading of the play. No one who has read the Bible or Augustine can doubt that hypocrisy and injustice dominate much of the world. That is simply one of the consequences of original sin. And in the context of the

play, the unjust rule because a king has vacated his throne and allowed
Scythians to fill the vacuum.

Even if critics do not, Lear's Fool recognizes that the turmoil in
the kingdom is a product of Lear's own folly. He summarizes the
orthodox position of the play in much the same way that Edmund
does at the beginning. When Lear calls him a "bitter fool," the Fool
offers to distinguish between the bitter and sweet fool:

> That lord that counselled thee
> To give away thy land,
> Come place him here by me;
> Do thou for him stand.
> The sweet and bitter fool
> Will presently appear:
> The one in motley here,
> The other found out—there. (1.4.138–145)

Lear catches his point: "Dost thou call me fool, boy?" And the Fool
admits it: "All thy other titles thou hast given away; that thou wast
born with" (1.4.146–148). Beneath Lear's other titles, beneath his
accommodations, Lear is, like all men, a born fool who once came
with a "wawl and cry" to the "great stage of fools" (4.6.180–184).

According to the Fool, however, Lear's inherent foolishness was
not alone responsible for his current state of "nothingness." Rather,
he was brought to this condition by a supreme act of folly:

> *Fool*: . . . Nuncle, give me an egg and I'll give thee two crowns.
> *Lear*: What two crowns shall they be?
> *Fool*: Why, after I have cut the egg i'the middle and eat up the meat,
> the two crowns of the egg. When thou clovest thy crown i'the middle,
> and gavest away both parts, thou borest thine ass on thy back o'er
> the dirt. Thou hadst little wit in thy bald crown when thou gavest
> the golden one away. (1.4.153–161)

The Fool adds that giving away the kingdom was like dropping his
pants to allow his daughters to spank him (1.4.169–170). If Lear is

getting dizzy, it is because he himself has turned the world upside down.

If the play is as rooted in deep comedy as I have claimed, then redemption must be possible in the world of *Lear*. It is—Edgar gets revenge on his brother and survives, and Gloucester, blinded though he is, has come to see things as they are. If redemption is possible, why is Lear not redeemed? Do we, in the end, have to fall back into an absurdist interpretation of the play? The answer to the last question is a firm "no." Lear is not wholly redeemed, to be sure, but only because he never wholly recognizes or acknowledges the extent of the damage he has caused. Act 4, scene 7 is a wonderfully touching scene of the reunion of Lear and Cordelia that one critic called the greatest comic scene in Shakespeare. It is day, Lear has slept and he is in new clothes; he is a *re*accommodated man. As he awakes, he speaks of being brought up from the torments of the grave: "You do me wrong to take me out o'the grave. Thou art a soul in bliss; but I am bound upon a wheel of fire" (ll. 45–47). He has been recalled to life, redeemed from the tortures of Hell or Purgatory, by Cordelia, his Beatrice.

More, the scene is an unutterably poignant recognition scene, which is simultaneously a reconciliation scene:

> *Lear*: Do not laugh at me,
> For, as I am a man, I think this lady
> To be my child, Cordelia.
> *Cordelia*: And so I am, I am.
> *Lear*: Be your tears wet? Yes, faith! I pray, weep not.
> If you have poison for me I will drink it.
> I know you do not love me, for your sisters
> Have, as I do remember, done me wrong.
> You have some cause; they have not.
> *Cordelia*: No cause, no cause. (4.7.67–76)

The daughter Lear had renounced is now, tenderly, "my child." When Lear confesses that Cordelia has some cause to hate him, Cordelia, who has identified herself with a theologically pregnant "I am," puts Lear's sin behind her, far as the east is from the west.

If Lear's only sin were against Cordelia, his death would be unjust in the extreme. Indeed, if Lear had done nothing but offend Cordelia, continuing the play for another act would be an artistic blunder of the highest degree. But Lear has done far more than offend Cordelia. He has favored two monstrous daughters who helped to promote Edmund, stepped aside from his public responsibilities, and led England into a dark age. It is impossible for Shakespeare to end the play here, impossible for him to ignore Lear's other sins. And so the play lurches on into further, and climactic, tragedy. Lear's divestiture has unleashed consequences that are not going to be stopped simply because of his reconciliation with Cordelia. Lear hopes to go away into a cage and spend his life in confinement with Cordelia (5.3.8–19), but this is just another way of expressing his original craven plan to crawl unburdened to the grave. Civil war, the plottings and machinations of Edmund, the invasion of France—these threats to the kindgom will not vanish simply because Lear loves his daughter again. Lear's deed, once done, cannot be undone.

This is not an absurd world, but exactly the opposite. It is a world where actions have consequences that are often far greater than the actors could have foreseen. But it is a world where the consequences flow from actions. This is simply a different world from that of Attic tragedy. And the "lesson" that it promotes is not a lesson of "tragic wisdom," or emotional exhaustion. It is the "lesson" that this world is ordered and will not brook assaults on its order.

As David Hart points out, *King Lear* is a tragedy taking place in a comic world, a story of death, loss, and waste made all the more painful for the real possibility of resurrection that occasionally shoots across the darkness. Hart's comment on the play serves as a wonderful concluding reflection on what tragedy means for Shakespeare:

> If one wanted to consider the difference that is wrought on tragedy by Christian culture, one might reflect upon the case of *King Lear*. Were *Lear* an Attic tragedy, it might well end upon the heath, at the

height of the protagonist's madness and at the point of his greatest and most demonic (that is, ennobling) despair, where he arrives at a final exhaustion of passion. Certainly there would not be the strange and beautiful reunion with Cordelia, overbrimming with imagery of resurrection and talk of forgiveness, because this scene of reconciliation (which strains after an eschatological hope) makes the subsequent death of Cordelia more terrible than anything in Attic tragedy: precisely because the spectator has been granted a glimpse of the joy that tragic wisdom is impotent to adumbrate—the restoration of the beloved—the death that follows is seen to be absolutely without meaning, without beauty, imparting no wisdom, resitant to all assimilation into any metaphysical scheme of intelligibility or solace.[10]

If ancient comedy is haunted by the fear of death, Christian tragedy is haunted by the hope of resurrection. A tragic vision of life makes ancient comedy sad; real hope of new life in the Christian comic view of things makes Christian tragedy all the more poignant.

III.

Twelfth Night illustrates "deep comedy" in two respects, which can be highlighted by attention to two main characters: Viola, who has been shipwrecked in Illyria and spends most of the play disguised as Cesario, a page boy employed by the Duke Orsino; and Malvolio, the steward of the house of the Countess Olivia. The story of Viola illustrates the comic trajectory toward resurrection and new beginnings; Viola's ultimate theme is, as she says, that "tempests are kind." Malvolio, humorless and oppressive, is the "devil" of the play and illustrates another side of deep comedy: the exclusion of the mirthless from final happiness and the power of jollity to defeat Satan. Satan, in the end, is overcome with nothing more than "cakes and ale."

Like most of Shakespeare's comedies, the plot of *Twelfth Night* turns on disguises, mistaken identities, and deceptions. In this play, the deceptions are multi-layered and complex. Most of the characters

[10] *Beauty of the Infinite*, 393, fn. 229.

are affected in one way or another by a deception or disguise, several because they are perpetuating deceptions but most because they are the victims. At the center of several of the deceptive plots is Sir Toby Belch, uncle to Olivia, the countess who is one of chief ladies of the play. From the beginning of the play and throughout, Toby is busy deceiving Sir Andrew Aguecheek, an absurd unknightly knight who is seeking to court Olivia. Toby tricks Andrew into believing that he is promoting his suit before Olivia, when in fact he keeps Andrew close to milk and bilk him. Andrew supplies the materials for the incessant parties and jollity of the house, and Toby would lose these funds if Andrew became convinced that Olivia would not have him. At the end, Sir Toby tells Andrew what he truly thinks of him: when Andrew asks him for help, he says that he is an "ass-head and a coxcomb and a knave, a thin-faced knave, a gull" (5.1.205–206). This is no recent opinion for Toby. Early on, he confides that "For Andrew, if he were opened and you find so much blood in his liver as will clog the foot of a flea, I'll eat the rest of the anatomy" (3.2.59–61).

In another scene, Toby perpetuates a more specific deception on Sir Andrew, convincing him to challenge Cesario (who, you will recall, is actually a woman, Viola, disguised as a page boy) to a duel and then filling Andrew with dread about Cesario's prowess with a rapier. Even more openly, Toby is one of the masterminds behind the gulling of Malvolio, the steward of Olivia's house. Together with Maria, a serving woman of the house, Toby leaves love letters for Malvolio to find, feeding Malvolio's pompous belief that Olivia is secretly attracted to him. The letter instructs Malvolio to smile, wear yellow stockings, and wear cross-garters—all of which is abhorrent to Olivia. In the main, Toby's deceptions and gullings have comic effects. He is the master of unrest, of jolly chaos, a Puckish practical joker whose plots never harm anyone seriously.

The other center of deceptions is Viola. Shipwrecked in Illyria and believing her brother Sebastian has died in the wreck, she disguises herself as a man and gains entry to Orsino's court. Orsino, sickening in his indulgent love for Olivia, enlists Cesario to visit the countess to press his suit. As a result, everyone in the house of Orsino is being fooled into believing that Cesario is a young man, and everyone in the house of Olivia is being fooled in the same way. This is similar to the women-disguised-as-men that we find in other Shakespearean comedies, but Viola's disguise is much more central to the plot and much longer-lasting. In *The Merchant of Venice*, Portia disguises herself for a few scenes in order to save Antonio from Shylock's attack. Imogen in *Cymbeline* is in disguise only for a time, as is Julia in *Two Gentlemen of Verona*. Further, in other plays the disguised woman has a confidant: Portia and Nerissa go to the court of Venice together, Imogen confides in Pisanio and in fact her disguise is Pisanio's idea in the first place. Viola is, by contrast, utterly alone. No one but she knows who she really is and what is really going on.

Given these circumstances, the effects of Viola's disguise are more various than the effects of Toby's pranks. At times, her disguise is exploited to ironic effect. In the first conversation between Orsino and Cesario/Viola, Orsino states his belief that Cesario will have better success wooing Olivia than "a nuncio of more grave aspect." Cesario is just the man for the job because of his womanly qualities:

> For they shall belie thy happy years
> That say thou art a man. Diana's lip
> Is not more smooth and rubious, thy small pipe
> Is as the maiden's organ, shrill and sound,
> And all is semblative a woman's part. (1.4.30–34)

By their second conversation, the audience already knows that Viola is falling in love with Orsino ("whoe'er I woo, myself would be his wife," 1.4.42), and this gives a painful depth to the conversation. Viola reminds Orsino that Olivia has every right to reject his suit, just as a woman would have to accept Orsino's rejection. Orsino objects that no woman could love as he loves:

> There is no woman's sides
> Can bide the beating of so strong a passion

> As love doth give my heart; no woman's heart
> So big to hold so much. They lack retention. . . .
> Mine is all as hungry as the sea,
> And can digest as much. Make no compare
> Between that love a woman can bear me
> And that I owe Olivia. (2.4.95–104)

Orsino speaks these words in the presence of a woman who has at least as strong a passion for him as he professes to have for Olivia. But all that Viola can do, disguised as she is, is to invent a "sister" who loved deeply and never professed her love:

> She never told her love,
> But let concealment, like a worm i' the body,
> Feed on her damask cheek. She pin'd in thought,
> And with a green and yellow melancholy
> She sat like patience on a monument,
> Smiling at grief. Was not this love indeed? (2.4.112–117)

Indeed it was, and it is the very love that Viola cannot speak. For her, "concealment" leads to sickly melancholy.

Even when Viola's disguise is used for somewhat more comic purposes, it quickly falls into this same bittersweet tone. While Viola is falling in love with Orsino, Olivia, believing Orsino to be a young man, has fallen in love with him/her. After their first encounter, Olivia sends her steward Malvolio after Viola to return a ring. Malvolio is multiply deceived here, and the joke is largely on him: he believes he is returning a ring to Orsino, but Orsino sent no ring; he believes he is communicating Olivia's rejection of a suitor, but he is actually playing pander as Olivia *pursues* a suitor (Cesario); and he believes that he is talking to a man, but he is talking to a woman. Witty as the scene is in making Malvolio a butt, it ends with a speech from Viola that can only be called a lamentation:

Disguise, I see thou art a wickedness
Wherein the pregnant enemy does much.

How easy is it for the proper-false
In woman's waxen hearts to set their forms!
Alas, our frailty is the cause, not we!
For such as we are made of, such we be.
How will this fadge? My master loves her dearly,
And she, mistaken, fond as much on me.
What will become of this? As I am man,
My state is desperate for my master's love;
As I am woman—now alas the day!—
What thriftless sighs shall poor Olivia breathe!
O Time! Thou must untangle this, not I;
It is too hard a knot for me t'untie! (2.2.28–42)

Here the potential for a tragic outcome is most acute, especially if Time does not prove an ally in untangling the knot that Viola's deception has caused. If Time is the tragic reality that the ancients, and many early moderns, believed, Viola's situation seems hopeless. But, as one critic put it, Shakespearean comedy in general is guided by a "faith," the conviction that man is perfectly capable of spoiling and ruining his world but absolutely incapable, on his own, of straightening it out. Something must come from outside human possibility; there must be an act of utterly surprising and undeserved grace, if potential tragedy is going to turn comic.

In *Twelfth Night*, Sebastian's reappearance is the outside intervention that eventually resolves Viola's dilemma, but as is frequent in Shakespeare the first move toward resolution has the effect of increasing confusion. The audience already knows Sebastian is alive from the middle of Act 3, since he appears there in conversation with Antonio, who has saved him from the shipwreck. Viola, however, has no suspicion that he is alive until after the duel scene. As Sir Andrew and Cesario, with keen reluctance on both sides, prepare to fight for the love of Olivia, Antonio sees the combat and intervenes to help, thinking he is intervening to help Sebastian, whom Viola, in her disguise as Cesario, closely resembles. Cesario of course knows nothing about Antonio, and she treats him kindly but as a stranger. Antonio is outraged at what he sees as ingratitude:

> But O how vile an idol proves this god!
> Thou hast, Sebastian, done good feature shame.
> In nature there's no blemish but the mind.
> None can be call'd deform'd but the unkind.
> Virtue is beauty, but the beauteous evil
> Are empty trunks, o'erflourished by the devil. (3.4.396–401)

Viola is stunned by the passion of Antonio's outburst, and by the fact that Antonio mistakes her for her supposedly dead brother. For the first time in the play, a glimmer of hope appears, hope that Viola expresses in some of the most exquisite lines in the play: "Prove true, imagination, O prove true, that I, dear brother, be now ta'en for you!" (3.4.406–407). And more fully:

> He nam'd Sebastian. I my brother know
> Yet living in my glass; even such a so
> In favor was my brother, for he went
> Still in this fashion, color, ornament,
> For him I imitate. O, if it prove,
> Tempests are kind and salt waves fresh in love! (3.4.411–416)

Time has begun picking at the knot. But not merely time; what makes tempests kind is grace, the grace of restored life, the grace of resurrection, the grace that rules tempests.

Once Sebastian appears in person, everything works out: Olivia's love for Cesario is (happily enough) transferred to a man, Sebastian, and Cesario's disguise is dropped to reveal a woman who can openly declare her love for Orsino. At the heart of the closing scene, though, is a deeply moving recognition whose emotional power cannot be captured on the page. It is beyond a recognition scene—it is a resurrection scene:

> *Sebastian:* Do I stand there? I never had a brother,
> Nor can there by that deity in my nature
> Of here and everywhere. I had a sister,
> Whom the blind waves and surges have devour'd.

Of charity, what kin are you to me?
What countryman? What name? What parentage?
Viola: Of Messline. Sebastian was my father;
Such a Sebastian was my brother too.
So went he suited to his watery tomb,
If spirits can assume both form a suit,
You come to fright us.
Sebastian: A spirit I am indeed,
But I am in that dimension grossly clad
Which from the womb I did participate.
Were you a woman, as the rest goes even,
I should my tears let fall upon your cheek,
And say, "Thrice welcome, drowned Viola." (5.1.230–245)

Past tenses ("I had a sister" and "Sebastian was my brother") become presents. Blind waves and surges have coughed up their prey, and the watery tomb has opened to Sebastian. All is redeemed. Every tear is wiped away, every loss restored, every wound healed. Tempests indeed are kind. We can hardly improve on Olivia's exclamation when she sees Cesario split in two: "Most wonderful!"

But it is not wonderful for everyone. *Twelfth Night* comes to a wonderfully comic conclusion for the main characters, but not for Malvolio. What shall we make of his exclusion from joy? At least we can say that "deep comedy" is not the same as "universalism." Deeply comic drama rights wrongs and turns lamentation to dancing, but it does not do so for everyone, particularly not for those who exclude themselves from joy. That is precisely what Malvolio does. Yet, Malvolio seems to receive far more abuse than he deserves, and his role in the play has to be explained in some fashion. Perhaps he is simply an error, Shakespeare nodding, the butt of a practical joke taken too far. But I think not. Not that Shakespeare is incapable of nodding; but Malvolio is too carefully worked through for his exclusion to be accidental.

Consider his name: *Malvolio* means "ill-willed," and such he is from his first appearance in the play, bantering with Feste, Olivia's fool.

Malvolio is not without wit, but he is wholly without humor, and Olivia, responding to Malvolio's insult of Feste, gets to the heart of his character: "You are sick with self-love, and taste with a distempered appetite" (1.5.96–97). To the extent that joy requires abandonment of self-love, to that extent Malvolio is without joy. His self-importance and self-love make him a perfect butt for jokes, but make it impossible for him to laugh at himself, to accept the exposure that is essential to comic redemption. Maria calls him a "Puritan," using the term not in its technical theological sense but in its already popular sense of a "kill-joy." More fundamentally, though, Malvolio is a "time-pleaser, an affectioned ass, that cons state without book and utters it by great swarths; the best persuaded of himself, so crammed, as he thinks, with excellencies, that it is his grounds of faith that all that look on him love him" (2.4.161–167). These descriptions color our impressions of Malvolio when we see his encounter with the revelers (2.3.86ff.). In the abstract, Malvolio's request that Sir Toby and his cohorts keep quiet at night is utterly reasonable. They are in fact wrong to make an "alehouse" of Olivia's house, and Malvolio is right, in the abstract, that they have no respect of place, persons, or time. Given the introduction we've had to Malvolio's character, we know that he would find an objection to *any* merry-making. He is a true Mal-volio.

Maria discerns that Malvolio's self-love and conceit make him a perfect target for the gulling. Even before he sees the counterfeit letter from Olivia, he is fantasizing about marriage to Olivia and what it would mean for him "to be Count Malvolio":

> Having been three months married to her sitting in my state. . . . calling my officers about me, in my branched velvet gown; having come from a daybed, where I left Olivia sleeping. . . . And then to have the humor of state, and after a demure travel of regard, telling them I know my place as I would they should to theirs, to ask for my kinsman Toby. . . . Seven of my people, with an obedient start, make out for him. I frown the while, and perchance wind up my watch, or play with my—some rich jewel. Toby approaches, curt-

sies there to me. . . . I extend my hand to him thus, quenching my familiar smile with an austere regard of control. . . . saying, "Cousin Toby, my fortunes having cast me on your niece give me this prerogative of speech. . . . You must amend your drunkenness" (2.5.48–79).

One of the most striking things about this fantasy is how little Olivia enters into it. She is lounging on a bed somewhere, perhaps, as Peter Saccio has suggested, exhausted from trying to keep pace with the sexual exertions of the oh-so-potent Malvolio. Malvolio's fantasy of marriage is only an excuse to lord it over Sir Toby. It is just an intensified version of his original sickness: he continues to be mortally sick with self-love.

This imagined future not only reveals his self-absorption but also reflects ironically on his supposed desire to keep the house in "good order," for there is nothing quite so disorderly as a steward who aspires to be lord of the manor. As a "lord of misrule," Sir Toby is a piker; Malvolio is the real master of chaos in the play. His self-absorption also manifests itself in his interpretation of the letter he finds. At first confused by the riddles and codes of the letter, he is determined to "make that resemble something in me" (2.5.131–132), and later he works out the riddle with these words: "to crush this a little, it would bow to me" (2.5.152–153). Maria has read her prey well: he's a solipsistic Procrustes who cuts everything to conform to his fantasies.

To see the full scope of Malvolio's role in the play, however, it is necessary to see how Shakespeare accumulates Satanic imagery around Malvolio. When he comes to Olivia smiling, wearing yellow stockings, and cross-gartered, Maria announces him by saying "He is, sure, possessed, madam" (3.4.9–10). Toby rushes in, acting as if Malvolio is the Gadarene demoniac: "If all the devils of hell be drawn in little and Legion himself possessed him, yet I'll speak to him" (3.4.96–98). When Malvolio tells Toby and Maria to "go off," Maria responds, "Lo, how hollow the fiend speaks within him" (3.4.103–104). Sir Toby rejoins, "How do you, Malvolio? How is 't with you?

What, man! Defy the devil. Consider, he's an enemy to mankind" (3.4.108–110), and Maria adds "An you speak ill of the devil, how he takes it at heart! Pray God he be not bewitched" (3.4.112–113). Toby tries once more, warning Malvolio not to "play at cherry-pit with Satan; hang him, foul collier" (3.4.129–130).

In a later scene, Feste, disguised as the cleric Sir Topas, comes to Malvolio's dark room to counsel with the wretched steward and to conduct a mock exorcism:

> *Malvolio:* Sir Topas, Sir Topas, good Sir Topas, go to my lady.
> *Clown:* Out, hyperbolic fiend! How vexest thou this man! Talkest thou of nothing but of ladies? . . .
> *Malvolio:* Sir Topas, never was man thus wronged. Good Sir Topas, do not think that I am mad. They have laid me here in hideous darkness.
> *Clown:* Fie, thou dishonest Satan! I call thee by the most modest terms, for I am one of those gentle ones that will use the devil himself with courtesy. Sayest thou that house is dark?
> *Malvolio:* As hell, Sir Topas. (4.2.26–39)

All this devilish imagery is part of the gulling, of course. But Shakespeare's imagery is not random. In particular, he frequently surrounds his villains with Satanic imagery. In *Othello*, for instance, Iago is described as a Satanic figure and uses hellish imagery himself. Over the course of that play, infernal imagery shifts from Iago to Othello himself, as Othello is slowly poisoned by the lies of the fiend. Likewise, in *Merchant of Venice*, Shylock is definitely identified as the villain of the story not only by his remorseless pursuit of the bloody bond, but also by the frequent use of Satanic imagery. Escaping Shylock's house, for instance, his daughter describes it as "hell," and the Christian who marries her performs a kind of harrowing. Thus in *Twelfth Night* the fact that Malvolio is called demon-possessed, and is associated with the devil over and over again, points to his thematic role in the play. Like Satan, he is sick with self-love, falling by the force of his own gravity, as Chesterton said. Of course, Malvolio is a *comic* devil, not nearly so threatening as Iago or Shylock, but he is a devil nonetheless.

And his devilry is manifest particularly in his desire to end the gaiety of Olivia's house. Here especially the title of the play comes into its own. *Twelfth Night* is named for the last night of the Christmas season, the final celebration of the Incarnation. It is a night for carnival, for suspension of the serious and structured. Malvolio wants to stop the merriment, and so it is fitting that he is ultimately excluded from it. But more: Malvolio is not only excluded from the comic climax of the play. He is excluded and overcome through trickery, practical joking, mirth. Satan digs a pit for the merry, but Satan falls into the very pit of merriment. And it tortures him forever.

In the final analysis, that is the practical import of all that has been said in this little book: the joy of Easter, the joy of resurrection, the joy of trinitarian life does not simply offer an alternative "worldview" to the tragic self-inflation of the ancients. Worked out in the joyful life of the Christian church, deep comedy is the chief weapon of our warfare. For in the joy of the Lord is our strength, and Satan shall be felled with "cakes and ale" and midnight revels.

Afterword

"Of the making of books there is no end." Solomon's bemused observation is usually taken to mean that there is always one more book to be written, if only because humans feel compelled to comment on the last book. But it applies equally well to individual books, at least to this book. Though this book is done (as is evident from the rapidly approaching back cover), it is still true that "of the making of *this* book there is no end."

If this book were brought to a real end, it would include at least two extensions. First, as I hinted in my discussion of *King Lear*, Christian literature not only produces deep comedy but also, and for precisely that reason, deep tragedy. Christian tragedy can no longer mean what ancient tragedy meant. There are still sad stories, but Christians cannot believe the world is not a sad story without abandoning their fundamental convictions about the triune God and the incarnation of the Son. Or so I have argued. But if the world is not a sad story, then the sad stories that remain are altogether sad because they need not be sad. So, I should add to this book a companion book on deep tragedy.

Second, the Christian possibility of comic resolution lends modern Western literature (particularly in the nineteenth and twentieth centuries) its particular power and intensity. Modern tragic literature (one thinks, for example, of Faulkner) adds to the noble resignation of ancient tragedy a post-Christian rage arising from frustrated expectations. Ancient tragedy knows nothing of a promise of redemption, and therefore can face the unredeemed world with a measure of equanimity. Oedipus pokes out his eyes, but before he dies he reaches a nearly divine calm at Colonus. Modern tragedy, by contrast, knows of the promise of the Christian God and His comic history, and is angry at Him for not being.[1] A post-Christian Oedipus will not stop with his eyes; he will throw himself in the river, thrust his harpoon at the white whale, die, go out and hang himself. Thus, the argument of this book could be extended into an analysis of modern literature, which is neither deeply tragic nor deeply comic, but deeply disappointed.

And, of course, if this book were to come to a real end, it would be much more thoroughly documented, more carefully argued, and more elegantly written. It would conform in every particular to the book of my imagination.

It is comforting that Solomon's quip about books occurs in Ecclesiastes. The whole point of Ecclesiastes, as I've argued elsewhere, is that our projects do not end even though we do. Deadlines (what an appropriate metaphor!) come and the book goes off, all unfinished, to press. Yet, Solomon says, that's okay; better than okay— it's a cause for gladness and feasting. And I have argued that it is better than okay because there is an end, the End, the endless End, when all will be well and all manner of thing will be well.

---

[1] I owe this insight to Randy Compton of Lee University, Cleveland, Tennessee.

Index